Th
o

MW00334729

The Lone Ranger on Radio, Film and Television

ED ANDREYCHUK

McFarland & Company, Inc., Publishers

Jefferson, North Carolina

ISBN (print) 978-0-7864-9972-4
ISBN (ebook) 978-1-4766-2971-1

LIBRARY OF CONGRESS CATALOGUING-IN-PUBLICATION DATA

BRITISH LIBRARY CATALOGUING DATA ARE AVAILABLE

Front cover: poster art for *The Lone Ranger and the Lost City of Gold*, 1958
(United Artists/Photofest)

Printed in the United States of America

*McFarland & Company, Inc., Publishers
Box 611, Jefferson, North Carolina 28640
www.mcfarlandpub.com*

Table of Contents

Introduction

*A fiery horse with the speed of light, a cloud of dust
and a hearty "Hi-yo, Silver!" The Lone Ranger!*
—narration from *The Lone Ranger* series, 1949–1957

Those were the opening lines of the popular television series that first excited me as a boy. I'll never forget him and his companion Tonto, righting injustices and then riding off on their horses, Silver and Scout. Making everything even more exciting was the music of *The William Tell Overture.*

From his debut on radio in 1933 to the most recent motion picture released in 2013, the Lone Ranger has withstood the test of time. Part of our entertainment culture for more than 80 years, like superheroes Captain America and Superman, he stands for "truth, justice and the American way." The TV series (1949–57) took a number of its stories from those originally written for the radio show created by George W. Trendle.

The radio show was still on the air during part of the TV run. In the late 1930s, two 15-chapter serials were filmed by Republic Pictures, *The Lone Ranger* and *The Lone Ranger Rides Again.* In the first, Lee Powell played the Lone Ranger. Robert Livingston was our hero in the latter. Chief Thundercloud played Tonto in both.

When the TV series *The Lone Ranger* began a decade later, Clayton Moore became the most beloved Lone Ranger of all. In the midst of the series' run, John Hart took over the part for a short time. Jay Silverheels played Tonto opposite both actors. Moore and Silverheels reprised their roles in a pair of motion pictures, *The Lone Ranger*, released by Warner Brothers in 1956, and *The Lone Ranger and the Lost City of Gold* released by United Artists in 1958. Moore and Hart also made guest appearances in character on other TV shows over the years, and Silverheels made a cameo appearance as Tonto in the 1959 Bob Hope comedy *Alias Jesse James.*

Animated programs for children were also seen on television. Clayton Moore continued wearing his costume, which included the mask, for personal appearances; and this caused problems with Jack Wrather, who by this time had taken over all Lone Ranger rights from George Trendle. This was especially evident when a new and younger Ranger and Tonto, played by Klinton Spilsbury and Michael Horse, came to the screen in Universal's 1981 feature *The Legend of the Lone Ranger.* It was more than 20 years before the Ranger appeared in another television production, and then 10 more before there was another feature film. Chad Michael Murray and Nathaniel Arcand played the Masked Man and Tonto in TNT's 2003 cable broadcast *The Lone Ranger.* The Disney film *The Lone Ranger* (2013) starred Johnny Depp as Tonto and Armie Hammer in the title role.

A number of entries in this book cover the Lone Ranger's origin. As John Reid, he joined his brother Dan, a Texas Ranger captain, and four other Rangers in pursuit of Butch Cavendish's outlaw gang. When the Rangers rode into a canyon called Bryant's Gap, they were ambushed and shot down by the outlaws. The only survivor was a badly wounded John Reid. Found by the Indian, Tonto, he was nursed back to health. Making a mask from Dan's vest, John became the Lone Ranger, determined to bring all outlaws to justice, aided by Tonto.

Pardon any shortcomings in this book, particularly in the chapter on the early history of the Texas Rangers. It is not in any way a definitive one, but only meant to capture highlights of some of the brave men and their obstacles in making the west a better place.

One

19th Century Texas Rangers

*No man in the wrong can stand against
a man in the right who keeps on a-coming.*
—William McDonald, one of the four
great Ranger captains

When Stephen Austin began colonizing Texas with settlers, it was still part of Mexico. For protection against marauding Indians, they formed a company of ten armed men. The commander was Lt. Moses Morrison.

Three months later, the summer of 1823, a proclamation by Austin used the word "rangers" to describe the company. This was the basis in 1998 for the 175th anniversary of the Texas Rangers. During the Texas Revolution, the first formal body, a Corps of Rangers, was created by the so-called Permanent Council. It was November 1835. Robert Coleman was chosen as the first Ranger captain. Three additional captains, John Tumlinson, Isaac Burton and William Arrington, were soon appointed. Their commander was Major Robert Williamson. Both Williamson and Burton were also privates in General Sam Houston's army in the last battle of the Revolution. It was fought at San Jacinto in April 1836; Texas won its independence from Mexico with the defeat of Santa Anna.

After Texas became a Republic, its first president was Houston. Sympathetic to the Indians, yet aware of the threat they posed, in December 1836 he helped establish a Ranger service for 280 mounted riflemen. Considered the strongest Indians on horseback, the Comanche also proved the strongest against Texans. Second Texas president Mirabeau Lamar wanted to annihilate any Indian threat. Those in line with Lamar's views included Colonel John Moore and his men, the most prominent Rangers of the late 1830s.

Texas Rangers first became the stuff of legend on June 8, 1844. Captain John "Jack" Hays was leading 14 men on a patrol looking for Comanche raiders. At Walker Creek, some 50 miles from headquarters in San Antonio, Hays' leadership earned him distinction as one of the best of all Ranger captains. Having his men take full advantage of their five-shot Colt revolvers, they beat back 70 warriors.

On December 29, 1845, Texas was annexed and became the 28th state. War between the United States and Mexico was inevitable, with Santa Anna returning to power. U.S. president James Polk, determined to protect the southernmost boundary of Texas on the Rio Grande, sent an army there in April 1846 under General Zachary Taylor. Assisting Taylor was a Ranger company led by Samuel Walker, who had been with Captain Hays at Walker Creek.

When Mexican lancers attacked, some of Walker's men were cut down. Sam Walker proved his courage on crucial scouting missions and became the Mexican War's first American hero. President Polk awarded him a commission as a regular army captain.

Included in the drive into Mexico with Taylor's army were Rangers under captains Ben McCulloch and Richard Gillespie, riding escort and guard. Officially part of Jack Hays' First Texas Mounted Volunteers, they were at the battle of Monterey in September 1846. Captain Gillespie was among those mortally wounded in the American victory.

After another win in Mexico City by the American forces the following year, Sam Walker and an advance guard were searching for the elusive Mexican commander Santa Anna. Walker was carrying the first authentic six-shooters, which he helped to create with Samuel Colt. Enemy resistance still threatened and Walker was killed in Huamantla fighting with his Colts.

The Rangers planned on killing Santa Anna when he was finally forced into exile. In April 1848, over 200 Rangers were on both sides of the road he would traverse. He was accompanied by his family and a military escort complete with clearly visible American flags. Seeing this, all the Rangers waited quietly until everyone passed and then went home.

In the last months of the Mexican War, Jack Hays' adjutant was John "Rip" Ford. When Hays later went to California, Ford replaced him as the most exemplary Texas Ranger captain fighting Indians throughout the 1850s.

Ford's most notable encounter was with Comanche raiders in the Indian Territory north of Texas. In command of just over 100 Rangers still in active service, he had additional support from an equal number of Indian allies. On May 12, 1858, having tracked the Comanches to their Antelope Hills camp, they defeated over 300 warriors. Killed in the fighting was Comanche chief Iron Jacket.

Mexican bandit Juan Cortina was then terrorizing the southern border of Texas. Cortina felt justified in attacking Brownsville in September 1859, after an old man was beaten by the marshal. When Rangers under William Tobin arrived a couple months later, a mob was incited and the old man was hanged.

Rip Ford was immediately sent there; ironically, the Rangers chose Tobin to command as Ford was a strict disciplinarian. Yet with only token support from Tobin, it was Ford and some 80 Rangers who chased Cortina back into Mexico. Governor Sam Houston then made sure Ford became senior officer for the rest of his Ranger service.

In 1860, Governor Houston realized his dream for a full Ranger regiment. But his choice of Middleton Johnson to administrate proved ill-advised; Johnson was overwhelmed by the logistics involved, and when things became too costly, the regiment was disbanded. Determined to have a Ranger presence on the frontier, Houston engaged Lawrence "Sul" Ross, a promising young Ranger and future Texas governor.

Texas Ranger glory was seen again on December 18, 1860, when Captain Ross and his Rangers, supported by cavalrymen, found another camp of Comanche raiders. In the ensuing battle at Pease River, the Indians were beaten. Ross killed Peta Nocona, their war chief, and took his wife and little daughter into custody.

Nocona's wife was revealed as Cynthia Ann Parker, who as a child in 1836 was abducted from her white family by the Comanches. Her daughter died from influenza, but a son became famous as Indian leader Quanah Parker.

During the Civil War (1861–1865), Texas joined the Confederate States of America. Having opposed Secession, Governor Houston was removed from office. While Rangers were still deployed in frontier defense against Indians, they were also assimilated into the Confederate army.

Surviving the Mexican War as a Ranger captain, Ben McCulloch became a Confederate officer and fought Union soldiers in Arkansas. In March 1862, he was killed at the battle of Pea Ridge.

His brother Henry McCulloch raised a Ranger regiment early in the war. Initially called the First Texas Mounted Rifles, by 1862 it was called the Frontier Regiment. One of its foremost Rangers was James "Buck" Barry, who was with Sul Ross when Cynthia Ann Parker was found.

James Bourland's Border Regiment also aided the frontier's defense in the war years. In October 1864, the most devastating Indian raiding involved this regiment of Rangers. Over 600 Comanches and Kiowas joined forces to attack settlers along Elm Creek, a tributary of the Brazos. Fourteen Rangers, led by Lt. N. Carson, managed to draw half of the Indians away, which allowed a number of the settlers to reach safety.

The last Indian struggle during the war occurred in early 1865 along a tributary of the Concho River called Dove Creek. Buck Barry sent 110 Rangers of the Frontier Regiment to help stop a far greater number of Kickapoos. With these Rangers were two militia units. They were still outnumbered; the situation proved a debacle for the Texans, and the Indians escaped.

Not until 1870 was Texas readmitted into the Union. The reasoning was that Texans found it difficult to cope with defeat and a new government following the Civil War. On June 13, 1870, to confront the unrelenting Indian danger, Governor Edmund Davis created 20 companies of Texas Rangers. It was only the second time in history those words were used in actual legislation; the first time was in 1866. Due to costs, however, only 14 companies saw service by year's end. They were called the Frontier Forces. Recognition was accorded to a number of companies and their captains. The commanders included Henry Richarz, Gregorio Garcia and David Baker.

Operating out of San Antonio, Captain Richarz struggled against the Kickapoos coming up from Mexico. Two of his Rangers were killed in a December 1870 Indian fight, including his own son Walter. Captain Garcia, whose Rangers were Mexican-Americans out of El Paso, fought Apaches coming from their strongholds in the Guadalupe Mountains. Perhaps Captain Baker and his men had the hardest task fighting both Kiowas and Comanches coming across the Red River from the north.

After army commander William Tecumseh Sherman came to Texas in May 1871, he decided the Indian trouble was a military matter.

Already been cut to seven companies because of costs, the services of the Frontier Forces were terminated a month later. When Richard Coke became governor in 1873, he supported Senator David Culberson's recommendation for a combined military and law enforcement force in Texas. Thus, on May 6, 1874, the Frontier Battalion was born, with Major John Jones chosen to command. Its six companies of mounted riflemen set into motion the great institution of Texas Rangers that exists today.

Although the U.S. military alleviated much of the Indian danger for the Frontier Battalion, it was still involved in about 14 Indian fights by December 1875. Also assisting the battalion in bringing law and order to Texas was a special force, the Washington County Volunteers. Led by Captain Leander McNelly, and actually referred to as McNelly's Rangers, this special force was initially set up in July 1874 by an adjutant general, William Steele. The reason was to deal with the worst feud in the state, which was between the Taylor and Sutton families of DeWitt County. A hired gunman for the Taylors was John "Wes" Hardin.

Hardin's later shooting of a lawman made him an outlaw. This was a contributing factor in Frontier Battalion captain Joe Waller's apprehension of more than 20 outlaws and cattle thieves. While Wes Hardin evaded capture, his brother Joe, mixed up in cattle fraud, did not. In June 1874, he was hanged by cattlemen in Comanche, Texas.

During 1875, Leander McNelly, stricken with tuberculosis, was replaced by Lee Hall of their newly titled Special State troops. Ranger John Armstrong was sent by Hall to track down Wes Hardin; on August 23, 1877, aboard a train in Florida, Armstrong coldcocked the outlaw with his Colt. Hardin served 16 years in prison and was then shot in the back of the head by a constable in El Paso.

Respective Ranger commanders John Jones and Lee Hall joined forces against another legendary outlaw, Sam Bass. On July 19, 1878, Bass and his gang planned to rob the bank in Round Rock, 20 miles from the Texas capital of Austin. With an informer's help, the Rangers were ready and Bass was badly wounded in a gun battle. Apprehended after briefly escaping, he then died from his wound.

In early 1879, John Jones began double duty as battalion commander and adjutant general. In November, Apache chief Victorio fled a New Mexico reservation with his followers. They raided in both Texas and Mexico. Jones had Lt. George Baylor assist U.S. cavalry and Mexican militia forces chase after the Apaches. For his efforts, Baylor received a captaincy in September 1880. On October 14, Victorio was killed by Mexican soldiers. Among the 78 other Indians slain, 18 were women.

Having left Victorio before this fatal encounter, a small number of Apaches attacked a stagecoach on a road to El Paso, killing all aboard. That was in January 1881; before the month ended, Captain Baylor and his men killed or arrested all the remaining Indians at their camp in Mexico's Diablo Mountains. Although regretting that the fatalities included women and children, the Texas Rangers realized this Indian fight was the last one.

During March 1881, cost reduction cut back the number of Rangers in the Frontier Battalion. John Jones managed to restore the battalion to six companies. It was with the addition of the recently terminated Special State Troops, which had been under the command of Lee Hall's replacement, Thomas Oglesby.

Due to a liver ailment, Jones died on July 18, 1881; his joint duties then became the responsibility of Wilburn Hill King. While remaining adjutant general, King gave temporary command of the Frontier Battalion to George Baylor.

Despite his past accomplishments as an Indian fighter, Baylor found the transition to law enforcer much harder. A battalion company under him in 1885 was one of two disbanded because of cutbacks; the other was in 1887.

There were always Rangers of merit. Along with Baylor, Ira Aten was involved in the Fence Cutting Wars of the 1880s. Barbed wire, used to fence off the once open range of cattlemen, was being unlawfully cut. Aten went undercover and even rigged dynamite charges to the fencing, which exploded if cut.

Sharing the glory for bringing the Texas Rangers through the remaining years of the 19th century and into a new one were John "Jack" Brooks, John Rogers, William McDonald and John Hughes. They became known as "the four great Ranger captains."

Jack Brooks joined the Rangers in 1883. Three years later, he was Rogers and Aten's formidable sergeant when they fought fence cutters together in Brown County, Texas. During an 1887 shoot-out with the Conner clan at Piney Woods, near the Louisiana border, Brooks lost a few fingers.

Made captain in 1889, he served with distinction until 1906. Joining

8

the Texas Rangers in 1882, Rogers differentiated himself from all the rest by his strong religious beliefs. He was also injured in the later Conner fighting, when he was shot in the left arm and side. Rogers served as Captain Brooks' sergeant for a time; his own distinguished tenure as captain was from 1893 to 1911.

William McDonald joined the Rangers as a captain in 1891. With his past experience as a lawman, he was the perfect choice to replace another prominent Ranger captain, Samuel McMurry. A captain until 1907, McDonald proved to be one of the bravest of all, whether handling labor disputes, chasing down killers, or performing any other duties.

Supported by Aten, Hughes became a Ranger in 1887. After his own captain, Frank Jones, was killed by thieves in 1893, Hughes took command of their company. Of the four great captains, he proved the ablest in leading men by example. A captain until 1915, he was the inspiration for famed author Zane Grey's character Buck Duane in the same year's novel, *The Lone Star Ranger*. The lone star became a symbol for Texans as early as 1836; George Childress, an original signer of the Texas Declaration of Independence, came up with the idea of a single star emblem. However, it was not until 1900 that the state first issued an official Texas Ranger badge, the five-pointed star in a wheel.

Ironically, that same year saw the end of the Frontier Battalion. It was after the state's attorney general decided that only commissioned officers, rather than all Rangers, could make lawful arrests.

But on March 29, 1901, the Texas legislature approved the proposal of then-adjutant general, Thomas Scurry, for a new Ranger force. While appropriations only allowed for four companies of 22 men in each, every Ranger had the authority to make arrests for the good of the service.

A new light was then lit which gave hope for the future success of the Texas Rangers. Leading these new companies were the four captains, Brooks, Rogers, McDonald and Hughes.

Two

Radio History

Other Texas Rangers all dead. You only Ranger left.
You lone Ranger now. —Tonto

On January 30, 1933, *The Lone Ranger* premiered on radio station WXYZ in Detroit, Michigan. Previously a CBS network affiliate, WXYZ was owned by George W. Trendle, who severed ties with the network to go independent. By doing so, he benefitted more financially from advertisers. His investment partner at the time was John H. King.

The station was instead losing money in 1932 when Trendle came up with the idea for a Western program. He envisioned its hero in the vein of a Zorro and Robin Hood. Trendle definitely wanted the hero to wear a mask and said, "I see him as a sort of lone operator. He could even be a former Texas Ranger."

With inspiration also derived from the Zane Grey book title *The Lone Star Ranger*, station manager Harold True exclaimed, "There's his name! The Lone Ranger."

During the first year the radio show was on the air, writer Fran Striker worked from his Buffalo, New York, home, mailing his Lone Ranger scripts to WXYZ. When the show became popular, he moved to Detroit and became the station's chief writer with his own staff.

As a freelance writer before, Striker had earlier been involved with Trendle and WXYZ on other radio programs, including *Warner Lester, Manhunter* and *Thrills of the Secret Service*. Prior to its WXYZ premiere, *The Lone Ranger* had a tryout in Striker's hometown of Buffalo on radio station WEBR. A local actor, John L. Barrett, played the title role.

The first actor to portray the Ranger at WXYZ was George Stenius. On May 9, 1933, he left to pursue a writing career. Later changing his last name to Seaton, he became a Hollywood writer-director. Among his movie credits were 1947's *Miracle on 34th Street* and 1970's *Airport.*

During Stenius' short run, Striker added Tonto so the Lone Ranger would not have to talk to himself or his horse. On February 25, 1933, the 12th episode, John Todd was first heard as the Masked Man's "faithful Indian companion."

Todd, who was born Fred McCarthy, was 56 at the time and known for his Shakespearean roles. Trendle later tried to replace him due to his age, but the replacement, an actual Native American, could not adjust to Tonto's broken English. The role was then returned to Todd. On the show's last live radio broadcast, September 3, 1954, he was the only remaining original cast member. In July 1957, he died at the age of 80.

When he initially portrayed Tonto, Todd was a member of the James Jewell Players, a repertory company used by WXYZ. Jewell came up with the Indian name Tonto ("Wild One") for Striker, also directed all the radio broadcasts for the first five years. In June 1938, he left to work at another radio station.

Charles Livingstone took over direction of the show until early in 1954, when George Trendle asked him to supervise the television series in California. During the live radio show's last months, Fred Flowerday was director.

Both Jewell and Bert Djerkiss, a WXYZ singer, were given credit for coming up with *The William Tell Overture* as the Lone Ranger's theme music. It was originally written by Italian composer Gioacchino Rossini for his 1829 opera *William Tell.* Other classical music was used, including Hungarian composer Franz Liszt's *Les Preludes* for bridging sequences. Perhaps no other music is so closely identified with a fictional character.

Apparently Jewell shared credit with Harold True for the Ranger's memorable call "Hi-Yo, Silver!" Initially it was the less formidable cry of "Hi-Yi," which had been written by Fran Striker in his earlier scripts.

Jewell was responsible too for the equally memorable "Kemo Sabe," the Indian name used by Tonto for the Lone Ranger. Translated as "Faithful Friend" on radio, then "Trusty Scout" on TV, the name came from a summer camp, Kee Mo Sah Bee, run by Jewell's father-in-law at Mullet Lake, Michigan.

Covered Wagon Days, a Western program heard earlier on Buffalo's

WEBR, was also written by Fran Striker. Striker, who adapted a number of those tales for his first Lone Ranger scripts, was responsible for the hero's trademark: the silver bullet.

Striker and his small group of writers had to adhere to Trendle's very specific guidelines regarding the Lone Ranger. They included he "never smokes, never uses profanity, and never uses intoxicating beverages"; he "uses precise speech, without slang, or dialect"; and he "never shoots to kill." The Lone Ranger was meant to symbolize courage, fair play and honesty.

After George Stenius departed, Lee Trent, under the name "Jack Deeds," and James Jewell stepped into the role for one night each (Trent on May 11, 1933, Jewell on May 13). Hired initially as a bit player the previous year by Jewell, Earle Graser began playing the Lone Ranger on May 16 at WXYZ. Three nights a week—Monday, Wednesday and Friday—Graser played the role for nearly eight years. At one point during the show's radio run, he was at a nightclub with his wife and there was a contest to see who could sound the most like the Lone Ranger. Not revealing who he was, Graser participated—and did not win. On April 8, 1941, he fell asleep at the wheel of his car and was killed in the resulting crash. He was 32.

During his years with the radio show, Graser did not make promotional appearances as the Ranger because of his slight stature. He did, however, appear in the role in a short-lived stage production in the Detroit area in the mid–1930s. Brace Beemer, who was taller, actually appeared publicly and in photos in Graser's place.

Beemer performed a number of jobs for the station over the years. He started as narrator on *The Lone Ranger* shortly after it began in 1933, and later served both as station manager and an actor. With Graser's death, Beemer was the perfect choice to take over the title role. For the next 13 years, until the final live broadcast, he played the part and became closely identified with it.

Yet the transition from Graser to Beemer was not immediate. So closely had Graser's own strong voice been part of the character that the change happened over five episodes, between April 9 to April 18, 1941. During this time, it was written that the Lone Ranger, hurt and bedridden from a gunfight, could barely speak above a whisper. When he did talk again, in a deeper voice than before, it was attributed to becoming even stronger in health.

Brace Beemer in his heyday as the voice of radio's Lone Ranger. He took the role quite seriously.

Long after Earle Graser was gone, his voice was heard calling "Hi-Yo, Silver! Away!" at the endings of both the radio and television shows.

The success of *The Lone Ranger* started on WXYZ, carried over to other Michigan stations, and kept growing at a phenomenal rate.

13

Just two months after its debut, it was being aired on WEN in Chicago, Illinois, WLW in Cincinnati, Ohio, and WOR in Newark, New Jersey. The show then became the springboard for the creation of the Mutual Broadcasting System in January 1934.

During January 1937, the show was first hooked up to the West Coast through the Don Lee network. Some 140 radio stations carried it by 1939, including outside the U.S. Transcripts were available for any station which did not carry it live.

Throughout its growth, Trendle never relinquished control of the show. He even had James Jewell sign over an "assignment of authorship" so the director-collaborator could not claim ownership on anything regarding the Lone Ranger.

Trendle also persuaded Striker to accept a small boost in pay rather than get a percentage deal; the chief writer's salary did increase handsomely over the years. Both Jewell and Striker certainly were a great part of the show's success. Striker and his writers wrote 156 radio adventures a year for the Lone Ranger and Tonto. It was estimated to about 60,000 words every week.

As a WXYZ writer, Striker was also involved on other radio shows, including *The Green Hornet*—which he favored. *The Green Hornet* was conceived by Striker and Trendle. Jewell and Charles Livingstone worked as directors on this show. Airing over the Mutual network from 1938 to 1952, it was a modern-day version of *The Lone Ranger*, with elements of the early *Batman* comics and movies. Britt Reid was a successful newspaper publisher, who with his faithful valet, fought crime incognito as the Green Hornet and Kato. They rode in a slick car called the Black Beauty.

Especially relevant here: The Lone Ranger's nephew, Dan Reid, Jr., was Britt's father. Dan's own father led the Texas Rangers in their fateful last ride against the Cavendish gang.

The Lone Ranger did not have automobiles like the Green Hornet or Batman to chase after the bad guys, but he did have his noble stallion Silver. Tonto's horses were Paint and Scout, the latter being the better known.

Probably with tongue in cheek, Brace Beemer claimed credit for coming up with silver horseshoes for the Ranger's steed. At the time of the radio show, Silver was also the name of the horse rode by Western film star Buck Jones. A number of ways were used on radio to make the sounds of the horses' hooves, including moving coconut shells and plungers over boards and sand.

Like the TV Masked Man Clayton Moore, Beemer was enthralled whenever he made a public appearance as the Lone Ranger. Beemer's white steed, which he rode extremely well, was named Silver Pride.

Trendle apparently did not allow any public appearances for some time following the first one in the summer of 1933. More than 70,000 fans, children and adults, broke through police barriers at a Michigan recreation area to get closer to the Lone Ranger. With the police not quite able to handle the situation, it was Brace Beemer who bravely came forth. Still in character, he quieted the fans by calling out, "Back Rangers! Back to your posts!"

The Lone Ranger remained part of the Mutual network until 1942, when it was briefly switched over to the NBC Blue Radio network. It 1943 it jumped to the ABC Radio network. John H. King, who had changed his last name from Kunsky back in 1936, was still a business partner with Trendle. H. Allen Campbell was responsible for bringing in advertisers for the show. The very first one was Silvercup Bread.

ABC Radio took over ownership of WXYZ in 1946 with the purchase of the King-Trendle Broadcasting Company. However, Trendle retained all rights to *The Lone Ranger*, as well as his other radio programs. That same year, Trendle entered another partnership, *with* Campbell but with*out* King.

Some 240 stations had aired *The Lone Ranger* when its radio run ended on May 25, 1956, with taped broadcasts. The final live broadcast in 1954 was its 2956th episode. As of October 2014, 973 episodes were available on the Internet through the OTR (Old-Time Radio) network.

Cast and crew are an essential part of any production and especially for a show that had the longevity of *The Lone Ranger*. Striker's writing staff included Ralph Goll, Felix Holt and Betty Joyce. As already noted, Bert Djerkiss assisted James Jewell with the exciting music (Djerkiss was also a sound effects technician with the show). Director Fred Flowerday worked with the sound effects team, which included Ted Robertson and Ernie Winstanley.

Winstanley also played young Dan Reid, the Ranger's nephew. Over the years, so did James Lipton and Bob Martin. For the 20th anniversary show, Martin was Dan, Jay Michael was his father Captain Reid, and Bill Saunders was villainous Butch Cavendish. Michael was also credited with playing Butch during the show's run.

Future movie star John Hodiak played a number of villains on the radio show. Director Charles Livingstone actually started out as an actor playing villainous roles, including in the early stage version. Among the show's female performers were Elaine Alpert, Bertha Foreman and Beatrice Leiblee. Along with Beemer, other announcers included Harold True and Fred Foy.

Foy began working as an announcer at WXYZ in 1942, but left to join the American armed forces during World War II. Returning to the station, he became both the last announcer and narrator on *The Lone Ranger* on July 2, 1948. He even played the title role once or twice.

His introduction for each episode became regarded as the most famous in the history of radio. Along with those immortal lines which opened this book's intro, Foy added, "Return with us now to those thrilling days of yesteryear. From out of the past come the thundering hoof beats of the great horse Silver. The Lone Ranger rides again!"

Three

The 1938 Serial
The Lone Ranger

*The dynamic hero of the airwaves,
now a dashing hero on the screen!*
—promotional copy used in 1938 newspapers

Released by Republic on February 12, 1938. 15 chapters; 264 minutes; black and white. From the radio serial by Fran Striker.

Credits:
Directors: William Witney, John English
Associate Producer: Sol C. Siegel
Supervisor: Bob Beche
Screenplay: Franklin Adreon, Lois Eby, Ronald Davidson, Barry Shipman, George Worthington Yates
Photography: William Nobles
Editors: Helene Turner, Edward Todd
Music Director: Alberto Colombo.

Cast:
Lynn Roberts [Lynne Roberts] (Joan Blanchard); Stanley Andrews (Mark Smith); George Cleveland (George Blanchard); William Farnum (Father McKim); Chief Thundercloud (Tonto); Hal Taliaferro (Bob Stuart); Herman Brix (Bert Rogers); Lee Powell (Allen King); Lane Chandler (Dick Forrest); George Letz [George Montgomery] (Jim Clark); John Merton (Kester); Sammy McKim (Sammy); Tom London (Felton); Raphael Bennet (Black Taggart); Maston Williams (Joe Snead); Frank McGlynn, Sr. (Abraham Lincoln); Charles Thomas (Blake); Walter James (Joe Cannon); Phillip Armenta (Dark Cloud); Forbes Murray (Marcus Jeffries); Jack Perrin (Morgan); Charles Whitaker (Perkins); Edmund Cobb (Rance); Silver Chief (Silver).

Chief Thundercloud as Tonto and Lee Powell as our masked hero, ready for action in this publicity pose for the 1938 serial.

CHAPTER 1 "Hi-Yo Silver!" 30 minutes, 17 seconds: In Pecos, Texas, outlaw Mark Smith impersonates tax official Colonel Marcus Jeffries after having him killed. When this new Jeffries begins to abuse his authority, Texas Rangers under Captain Rance are sent to investigate. Aided by henchman Joe Snead, Jeffries and his so-called troopers ambush the Rangers in a canyon and shoot them down. Tonto finds one survivor badly wounded and cares for him in a cave. The man, whose identity is known only to Tonto, swears an oath to avenge the deaths of his comrades. Wearing a mask and riding his white horse Silver, he becomes the Lone Ranger. Suspecting that the Lone Ranger is one of five men, Snead has them locked up at the stockade. Their names are Bob Stuart, Bert Rogers, Allen King, Dick Forrest and Jim Clark. One man reveals his masked identity to the other four, and they decide to band together in the spirit of Rangers. When Federal administrator

From the 1938 serial, a quintet of actors in a striking pose. Left to right, top row: George Letz (a.k.a. George Montgomery) and Lane Chandler. Bottom row: Lee Powell, Herman Brix and Hal Taliaferro.

George Blanchard arrives with his daughter Joan, their coach is used by Tonto to help the Rangers to escape. As the other Rangers are pursued, the Lone Ranger returns to the stockade with Tonto to help ranchers caught inside. Losing the gate's key, Snead lights a fuse to blow it open. In the ensuing chaos, the Lone Ranger is knocked to the ground.

CHAPTER 2 "Thundering Earth," 18 minutes, 22 seconds: The gate explosion kills Joe Snead. Inside the stockade, ranchers rush to join the Lone Ranger against the troopers. The Ranger beats trooper captain Kester in a fistfight. Back in Pecos, local priest Father McKim convinces George Blanchard that Jeffries should be arrested. All the ranchers are being threatened by Jeffries' troopers. As the Lone Ranger arrives to help, an explosion causes an avalanche.

19

CHAPTER 3 "The Pitfall," 16 minutes, 43 seconds: With rocks coming down toward him, the Lone Ranger cannot stop Blanchard and Joan from being captured by Jeffries. Joan's father is forced to give Jeffries Federal authority as magistrate. Joan warns the Lone Ranger about a letter being prepared, against her father's will, to give Jeffries both military and governmental control. As Joan escapes from Jeffries, Tonto and the Lone Ranger attempt to get the letter. Aware of a pit with sharp stakes devised by Jeffries, the Lone Ranger races on Silver after Joan to keep her away from this danger. The Ranger and Joan fall toward the pit.

CHAPTER 4 "Agent of Treachery," 16 minutes, 39 seconds: Joan lies clear of the pit while the Lone Ranger hangs at its edge. But he climbs free and then destroys the letter, spoiling Jeffries' plans. Black Taggart, another outlaw, is then used by Jeffries to lure the five Rangers into a trap. The Lone Ranger gets the upper hand by switching clothes and masquerading as Taggart. From hiding, one of the troopers throws a rock at the actual Ranger.

CHAPTER 5 "The Steaming Cauldron," 16 minutes, 17 seconds: Knocked down by the rock, the Lone Ranger is helped by Tonto and they escape from the troopers. In Pecos, Joan mistakes Taggart, still in the Ranger's outfit, for the real Lone Ranger and gives him a message. Taggart uses this to his advantage by having Father McKim send a different message for the Rangers to meet Joan and her father at a nearby mill. The mill turns out to be the place where Jeffries stores his gunpowder. The five Rangers battle there against the troopers, destroying some of the powder. In the process, Jim Clark is shot by Taggart.

As the injured Ranger returns to the hidden cave, Taggart follows. The Lone Ranger appears and fights Taggart, who gets stuck in a crevice over a steaming sulfur pit. Freeing his adversary, the Lone Ranger is instead pulled into the crevice.

CHAPTER 6 "Red Man's Courage," 16 minutes, 28 seconds: Trying to escape, Taggart is stopped by Silver and falls into a pit to his death. Silver helps the Lone Ranger get out of the crevice. The Ranger races to the wounded Jim Clark and is at his side when he dies. In yet another scheme, Jeffries hires Blake and Perkins to kill two Comanche Indians. When silver bullets planted near the bodies are found by Chief Dark Cloud, the Lone Ranger is blamed and Tonto is taken captive. A bound

Tonto is to be burned at the stake by the Comanches. With flames all around his Indian companion, the Lone Ranger arrives to help him and falls from his horse.

CHAPTER 7   "Wheels of Disaster," 15 minutes, 58 seconds: Getting to his feet, the Lone Ranger saves Tonto from the fire. Soon they are cleared when lead bullets are found in the slain Indians. Sneaking up on the Comanche camp, Blake is injured by Silver. When Perkins is captured, he blames his partner for the killings; then shooting him down, Blake succumbs too from his own injury. As Jeffries has his troopers make off with wagons of gunpowder, he places Joan in one of them. Not knowing she is aboard, ranchers try to stop the wagon by blowing it up. The Lone Ranger gets to the wagon after a wild chase, but it suddenly explodes when hit by a bullet.

CHAPTER 8   "Fatal Treasure," 16 minutes, 54 seconds: Joan and the Lone Ranger escape in the nick of time. She is again taken captive by Jeffries. A cavalry unit arrives in Pecos for the silver money collected by Jeffries as taxes. He intends to steal it, Joan alerts the Lone Ranger, who hides the silver in a well where he can later retrieve it with his three comrades. Two are caught inside the well by Jeffries' troopers. Captain Kester uses a cannon to then blast it.

CHAPTER 9   "The Missing Spur," 16 minutes, 35 seconds: While the cannon blast destroys the well, the two Rangers climb free from another one. Kester is briefly held by them as a guarantee of safety out of Pecos. As Jeffries has the Rangers chased down, they draw his men off to allow time for Tonto to hide the silver. The cavalry then capture and jail all the Rangers in the belief that they stole the silver. With Tonto's help, the Lone Ranger escapes, losing a spur in the process. Returning the silver to the cavalry, the Ranger is back in jail with his comrades, unmasked, when Kester arrives. The captain is certain that he only has to look for the man with the missing spur to reveal the identity of the Lone Ranger.

CHAPTER 10   "Flaming Fury," 16 minutes, 33 seconds: Kester is surprised when all four Rangers have a missing spur. Although freed of the Federal charge of stealing the silver, the Rangers still need to escape jail. Meantime, Joan is forced into a marriage ceremony with Jeffries to save her father's life. The Lone Ranger arrives in time to prevent it. Forced to flee from Jeffries' men, Tonto and the Lone Ranger take shelter in a barn. When their adversaries start a fire, the two appear trapped.

CHAPTER 11 "The Silver Bullet," 16 minutes, 18 seconds: As the burning barn collapses, the Ranger and Tonto hide beneath a trapdoor. Jeffries brings in an outlaw called Morgan to get the Lone Ranger. Joe Cannon, who is Ranger Bob Stuart's uncle, is killed by Morgan while casting the Lone Ranger's silver bullets. Cannon's grandson Sammy is sent by Bob to the cave for the other Rangers. Showing two silver bullets in a Pecos cantina, Stuart gets into a gunfight with Morgan and his cronies. While taking down Morgan's men, he is badly injured. Morgan, thinking Stuart is the Lone Ranger, is ready to finish him off with a shotgun.

CHAPTER 12 "Escape," 16 minutes, 22 seconds: The real Lone Ranger suddenly appears and drops Morgan with his pistols. With troopers all around, the only escape is through a trapdoor to the roof. Bob Stuart succumbs to his wounds. Finding a wanted poster for Mark Smith, Joan realizes his masquerade as Jeffries and informs her father. Smith retaliates by sending them both on a coach ride with the sole purpose of having them killed. The Lone Ranger fights off their guards, then drives the coach away with father and daughter still inside and with Smith's men in hot pursuit. Going around a sharp mountain pass, the coach spins out of control and heads toward the edge of a steep cliff.

CHAPTER 13 "The Fatal Plunge," 16 minutes, 37 seconds: The Blanchards and the Lone Ranger jump safely from the coach. One of Smith's henchmen, Felton, is captured by the Ranger and taken back to the cave. Around a campfire, a number of incidents that have already occurred are discussed by the three Rangers, the Blanchards, Sammy and Tonto. Felton escapes to a high ledge inside the cave. Ranger Dick Forrest climbs behind Felton in an effort to recapture him. Leaping to him on the ledge, Forrest and Felton both topple off.

CHAPTER 14 "Messengers of Doom," 16 minutes, 49 seconds: The fall from the ledge kills Felton and injures Forrest. Seeing Father McKim's carrier pigeons flying about, and suspecting he is in danger, Tonto, Allen King and Bert Rogers go to his assistance. Kester uses the pigeons to find the hidden cave. Forrest then sends Sammy and the Blanchards to a safer part of the cave. Shot by Kester's men, Dick shoots at the cave's ceiling, causing the stalactites to come crashing down just as the Lone Ranger arrives.

CHAPTER 15 "The Last of the Rangers," 17 minutes, 3 seconds: Kester and his men are killed by the falling stalactites while the Lone Ranger escapes the danger. Dick Forrest dies in the struggle. When Mark Smith and his remaining men assault the cave's occupants, the two Rangers go for more ammunition.

Silver follows them as one Ranger is shot down. The other man becomes the Lone Ranger. Many ranchers are brought back by the Lone Ranger to defeat the troopers. While Tonto prevents Smith from escaping, the Lone Ranger and his adversary seem to fall from a cliff to their deaths. As a funeral service is held for the five brave Rangers, the Lone Ranger appears, having survived the fall. At Joan's request, he reveals his identity as Allen King. Then the Lone Ranger and Tonto ride off together.

My father and I shared a love for Westerns. As a boy of nine going on ten, he first saw 1938's *The Lone Ranger*. Years later he would become excited remembering the serial for me when it was considered a lost film. Especially vivid was his memory of the remaining two Rangers riding out for more ammo in the last chapter; and when one was killed, my dad still did not know which man until the final unmasking.

In June 1937, a contract was signed by George Trendle allowing Republic Pictures to make a 15-chapter serial followed by a condensed version of the same production. The results were *The Lone Ranger* in 1938 and a 69-minute feature, *Hi-Yo Silver*, released on April 10, 1940. In between, there was another 15-chapter serial, 1939's *The Lone Ranger Rides Again*.

Budgeted at $160,315, the first serial went over by $7802, making it the costliest one at the time for the studio. Its initial 19-day shooting schedule was the shortest of any other Republic serial, but filming actually took place from November 28 to December 31, 1937. Most of the exterior action scenes, directed by William Witney and John English, were filmed in Chatsworth, California, at the Iverson Movie Ranch.

Additional outdoor work was done near Lone Pine, California, in the Alabama Hills and with Mount Whitney in the background.

Although *The Lone Ranger* was very successful at the box office, and created even more interest in the radio show, Trendle was not entirely pleased with the end results. He did not carp at the initial $18,750 paid by Republic for the rights, nor the ten percent of the theater rentals earned for the serial above $390,000; Trendle's dismay was due to the studio's concept of one of five men, united as Rangers, being the Lone Ranger, and the actual one revealing his true identity.

Ironically, this different concept only enhanced the Lone Ranger legend with its excitement and mystery. "A landmark in the history of the serial," was what it was accurately called by Phil Hardy in his book *The Encyclopedia of Western Movies*. Barry Shipman, George Worthington Yates, Franklin Adreon, Ronald Davidson and Lois Eby were Republic's team of credited writers on the serial. At least four of them actually spoke with Fran Striker in Detroit before starting work on the screenplay. What advice was offered by Striker was never revealed. Assuredly the masked rider of the plains, Tonto, Silver and the silver bullets were all accounted for in the great fight for justice.

Trendle and Striker both liked the Lone Ranger origin created for the serial by uncredited screenwriter Oliver Drake, and used it for their radio show. Instead of the serial's Mark Smith leading the ambush against Captain Rance's Texas Rangers, it was Butch Cavendish attacking Captain Reid's men. Trendle also liked Alberto Colombo's music direction on the serial and incorporated some of his themes for the radio show.

Republic's top serial directors John English and William Witney worked as a team during the 1930s and 1940s. Their serials included 1937's *Zorro Rides Again*, 1939's *Zorro's Fighting Legion* and 1941's *King of the Texas Rangers*. They also collaborated on *The Lone Ranger Rides Again*. Separately, English worked on the *Gene Autry* and *Roy Rogers* TV shows in the early 1950s; his last Western credit was for a TV episode of *Laredo* in 1966.

Witney's TV credits included many episodes of the Disney series *Zorro* in the late 1950s and many *Bonanzas* during the 1960s. His final Western credit was a 1968 episode of *The High Chaparral*. In his 1996 autobiography *In a Door, Into a Fight, Out a Door, Into a Chase: Moviemaking Remembered by the Guy at the Door*, Witney wrote of the 1938

Lone Ranger, "I don't think a more handsome group of men were ever assembled together in one picture." The director was referring to the five actors (Lee Powell, Herman Brix, Lane Chandler, Hal Taliaferro and George Letz [George Montgomery] who made such an outstanding team. Any one of them could have passed muster as the Lone Ranger.

When the serial came out, ads proclaimed, "Featuring the Lone Ranger, a Man of Mystery." None of the men playing the Texas Rangers had their names included in these initial ads. During the course of the serial, no one Ranger appeared to be the leader of the group with all dispensing orders or advice equally. This made the guessing game ("Which is the Lone Ranger?") more intriguing as all five also dressed alike and were of similar size.

In the years ahead, George Montgomery Letz became the best known of the five actors after he began using his middle name for his last. But in *The Lone Ranger* he was the first to die as Jim Clark. His death in Chapter 6 is very moving as his comrades stand side by side at his grave, and Tonto sings to the sunset.

Both Montgomery and his character were the youngest of the group. Born in 1916, the actor was just 21 when he appeared in the serial. The name change to George Montgomery came in 1940 when he left Republic for 20th Century–Fox. While there, he became a leading man in a variety of films, with a number of top actresses of the day including Betty Grable and Maureen O'Hara.

After leaving Fox, the Western genre especially fit his rugged and handsome persona. Having already starred in a 1950 feature called *Davy Crockett, Indian Scout,* as the frontiersman's nephew, Montgomery was considered in 1954 for the title role in Disney's TV production "Davy Crockett King of the Wild Frontier." During the 1958–59 television season, Montgomery starred as Mayor Matt Rockford in his own Western series, *Cimarron City.* Guest starring in one episode was his then wife, singer-actress Dinah Shore; they were married from 1943 to 1962. Montgomery died in December 2000 when he was 84 years old.

Floyd Taliaferro Alderson, born in 1895, was the oldest (42) of the five Rangers. Billed first among them in the serial, as Hal Taliaferro, his character of Bob Stuart bravely yet perhaps recklessly seals his fate in Chapter 11 when he singlehandedly takes on the cantina full of gunmen.

The actor first made his mark in silent films beginning in 1924 for the Pathe Company, which billed him as Wally Wales and made him a "B" Western star. He continued his stardom as Wales when sound came along for the Big 4 Film Company and in the 1930s for Imperial Pictures.

The final name change to Hal Taliaferro came in 1936 and with it a change from starring roles to character roles. He played Jim Bowie in Republic's 1937 serial *The Painted Stallion*; as Old Leather, he rode with John Wayne in the 1948 Western classic *Red River*. *Law of the Lawless* (1964) with Dale Robertson was his last Western film. Taliaferro died at age 84 in February 1980.

Born in 1899, Robert L. Oakes was four years younger than Hal Taliaferro. Oakes changed his name in 1923 to Lane Chandler and became a Paramount star until the sound era rolled in and another actor took his place: Gary Cooper. Both actors were tall and had amiable personalities. Chandler appeared in a few of Cooper's films, including 1936's great Western *The Plainsman*.

Before he played Dick Forrest in *The Lone Ranger*, Chandler was seen as Davy Crockett in Republic's 1937 feature *Heroes of the Alamo*. Chandler later appeared on the *Lone Ranger* TV series and the 1956 feature film. A 1964 TV episode of *Wagon Train* was his last Western credit. In September 1972, he passed away at 73.

The fates of Chandler and Herman Brix's Bert Rogers are sealed in the last chapter. The camaraderie and sacrifice shown by all five Rangers is fully appreciated by the time Brix and Lee Powell's Allen King take their last ride together for more ammunition after wishing each other good luck.

Born in 1906 with the first name Harold (Herman was his middle name), Brix was 31 when he played perhaps the most laid-back of the comrades. An accomplished athlete, he represented the U.S. at the 1928 Olympic Games and won the silver medal in the shot put.

Herman Brix's fine physique undoubtedly helped him win the role of Tarzan in 1935's serial *The New Adventures of Tarzan*. Apparently not satisfied with the way his film career was evolving, Brix took acting lessons and changed his name to Bruce Bennett in 1939.

Supporting roles for the actor then followed at Warner Brothers including his best one with Humphrey Bogart in 1948's *The Treasure of the Sierra Madre*. In 1956, Bennett was again at Republic starring in

Daniel Boone, Trail Blazer. Two 1967 TV episodes of *The Virginian* were his final Western credits. When he died in February 2007, Bruce Bennett was 100.

The actor who portrayed the first Lone Ranger in films lived a short life. Enlisting in the U.S. Marine Corps during World War II, Lee Powell was just 36 when he died of alcohol poisoning while his unit was deployed on the island of Tinian in 1944.

His Lone Ranger is a vibrant hero. While a good portion of the action performed in the serial was done by two incredible Hollywood stuntmen, Yakima Canutt and Ken Cooper, Powell and his fellow Rangers nonetheless cut splendid figures.

Born in 1908, Powell was 30 at the time of *The Lone Ranger* and the next youngest of the five men after Montgomery. "Believe it or not," Lee wrote in a November 1938 article for *Good Housekeeping* magazine, "it was the first picture job I ever had." Proud of his contribution, he made public appearances billed as the actor who played the Lone Ranger—until Republic stopped him.

Powell and Herman Brix co-starred in another 1938 Republic serial, *The Fighting Devil Dogs*, also directed by Witney and English. In 1942, Powell played a character named Peter Stewart in six "B" Western films with Bill "Cowboy Rambler" Boyd.

The actor summed up the success of *The Lone Ranger* rather nicely in that same *Good Housekeeping* feature: "The mask and the mysterious hero surely was one reason. The cry 'Hi-Yo, Silver' was another. Many people, and youngsters particularly, got a thrill out of seeing a moving picture that really moved with speed. Fast riding. Fast shooting. Fast punching."

The dynamics of the riding and fighting between the Lone Ranger and his adversaries made the action special. My favorite sequence is in Chapter 12 when he rescues the heroine and her father trapped in the coach. With a passel of bad hombres hot on their tail, the *William Tell Overture* creating even more excitement, and the Lone Ranger driving away atop the coach at breakneck speed, it is breathtaking.

The masked hero was played in those thrilling sequences, according to director Witney, by Yakima Canutt. William Witney told an amusing story in his autobiography about this top stuntman: "Yak always had a chaw of tobacco tucked in one cheek, and at odd times had to get rid of it in the usual five-foot stream. He got so used to wearing the mask that he'd forget to lift the bottom half before ejecting the five-foot stream."

Enos Edward Canutt, born in 1895, was a professional rodeo performer and earned the title of World's Best Bronco Buster at 17. After getting a taste of Hollywood in 1919, he became both a stuntman and actor in silent films. He perfected the Crooper Mount, a jump over the horse's backside and into the saddle seen in many Westerns. Canutt also later invented the "Running W," used in horse falls for *The Lone Ranger* and other Westerns: leather hobbles were buckled to the front legs of a horse between hoofs and fetlocks. A cable was then secured to the hobbles and when it ran out as the horse galloped off, both animal and rider tumbled forward to the ground.

While no horses were injured during the making of the serial, two animals were later killed in a film using the "Running W." (Canutt was not involved.) However, this caused the Humane Society to ban the stunt. In his autobiography, Canutt was very forthright: "In my 50 years of handling action in the picture business, I have only lost two horses," he said, "one was a runaway who crashed into a tree and broke his neck, and the other broke a leg on the ice in a sleigh chase."

Two of Yakima's most celebrated films as a stuntman were both in 1939. In *Gone with the Wind* he doubled Clark Gable, and in *Stagecoach* he doubled Andy Devine and John Wayne. Another great film was 1959's *Ben-Hur*, where he directed the action for the chariot race. The famed stuntman and action director died at age 90 in May 1986.

While *The Lone Ranger* was being made, Republic decided to substitute another man's voice for the masked man. This was done so the actor seen on film in the role—in this case, Lee Powell—would not be readily recognized by his own voice as his identity was to remain a secret until the serial's conclusion. The mask fully covering the face eliminated the need to lip-sync.

Five actors were sent to the Iverson Ranch location and all called out "Hi-Yo, Silver! Away!" for director Witney. One was a standout: According to the director, his booming voice "echoed across the valley for what seemed like five minutes." The actor, Billy Bletcher, was only 5'2" and weighed 200 pounds but his voice proved perfect for the role of the Lone Ranger.

Bletcher was perhaps best known at the time for his voice work in animated films. In Disney's 1933 *Three Little Pigs*, he was the Big Bad

Wolf. Republic used his voice talents again in *The Lone Ranger Rides Again* and as a Yaqui Indian god in *Zorro's Fighting Legion*. On the *Lone Ranger* radio show in 1950, Bletcher was heard as several different characters. He also appeared as a character in a 1950 episode of the TV series, "Gold Train." At 84, Bletcher passed away in January 1979.

In Chapter 1 of *The Lone Ranger*, a shadow is seen against a canyon wall after Captain Rance and his men are killed. The shadow is revealed as Tonto, who looks toward the heavens when he finds one survivor.

Hollywood turned Victor Daniels, born in 1889, into Chief Thundercloud (also spelled Thunder Cloud) for the movies. Along with his playing Tonto in both the 1938 and 1939 serials, the actor's film career was dominated by Indian roles until his death in November 1955 when he was 66 years old.

His first appearance in a major Western was as Sitting Bull in 1935's *Annie Oakley* with Barbara Stanwyck. For 1939's *Geronimo*, he was given the title role. The final Western film of his career was 1952's *Buffalo Bill in Tomahawk Territory* with Clayton Moore.

As Tonto in the serials, Thundercloud set the standard for the Indian's appearance, which was continued by Jay Silverheels in the TV series. They indeed looked similar with their headbands and buckskin costumes. Even their hairstyles matched. (Moore's Lone Ranger outfit differed a bit from those of his serial counterparts Powell and Bob Livingston.)

If the year of her birth, 1922, is accurate, Theda Mae Roberts was only 16 when she played in *The Lone Ranger*. Another source mentions 19 as her age. As pert heroine Joan Blanchard and billed as Lynn Roberts, she certainly seemed more mature than her years. She was very graceful and charming in her role.

Also in 1938, as Lynne Roberts, with an "e" added to the end of her first name, the actress played in another Republic serial, *Dick Tracy Returns*, and it too was directed by the team of English and Witney. Twenty-one of her 64 films were Westerns and included two with George Montgomery and seven with Roy Rogers in 1938 and 1939.

Her fate, like that of co-star Lee Powell, was a sad one. At home in late 1977, she fell and hit her head on the floor, then lapsed into a coma. She died in April 1978 at the age of 55.

Roberts helped to make *The Lone Ranger* a memorable experience.

At the very end, when she asks our hero to remove his mask, she then warmly says the name "Allen King." "Till we meet again," he responds before riding away with Tonto at his side.

Quite good as George Blanchard, Joan's devoted father, was that fine character actor George Cleveland. This is most apparent in Chapter 3 when he cries out in anguish when his daughter's life is threatened by despicable villain Mark Smith.

Cleveland's versatility was again proven in the 1948 Western *Albuquerque*, where he was the main villain tormenting Randolph Scott and an entire town. He appeared with George Montgomery in another Western, 1952's *Cripple Creek*. However, as the beloved Gramps on the *Lassie* TV series from 1954 to 1957, George Cleveland received his greatest career recognition. When he died in July 1957 at 71, the actor had appeared in 116 episodes of the series.

Another beloved TV character, the Old Ranger hosted the long-running Western anthology series *Death Valley Days* between 1952 and 1963. He was played with tremendous dignity by Stanley Andrews. In *The Lone Ranger*, Andrews' versatility as a character actor made for one of the great serial villains. As Mark Smith impersonating Marcus Jeffries, he was capable of any cold-blooded, calculating act, including murder, in his mad grab for power. Many good men meet tragic ends due to his actions and those of his slimy cohorts.

Born Stanley Andrzejewski in 1891, his first major acting role was Daddy Warbucks on the *Little Orphan Annie* radio show from 1931 to 1936. Among his many Western television credits were seven episodes of the *Lone Ranger* series between 1949 and 1955. When he died in June 1969, Andrews was 77.

The first of Smith's henchmen to bite the dust in the serial, after arranging the ambush of Captain Rance's Texas Rangers, is Joe Snead. He personally shoots down the captain. Snead's demise is ironically caused by his own hand when he blows up the stockade gate to close out the first chapter. Playing the dastardly double-crossing Snead was Maston Williams, who was born in 1879 and joined up with Republic Pictures at its inception in 1935. He made his last movie in 1939. At the age of 99, he died in July 1978.

After fatally wounding Jim Clark in Chapter 5, henchman Black Taggart's (Ray Bennett) demise is caused by the Lone Ranger's horse Silver, in the next chapter: Taggart falls into the sulfur pit when the great stallion rears up on its hind legs. Born in 1895, Bennett had over 150 film and television credits to his name. He was seen in one *Lone Ranger* TV episode in 1949 and two in 1950. When he played Black Taggart in the 1938 serial, the actor was billed as Raphael Bennett. He died at 62 in December 1957.

Lynn Wakefield Perrin, born in 1896, began acting in silent films in 1917. Twenty years later, having carved a niche for himself in "B" Westerns using the first name Jack, he was Davy Crockett in Republic's serial *The Painted Stallion*. In December 1967, he died at age 71.

As gunman Morgan in *The Lone Ranger*, Jack Perrin is responsible for the fates of both Bob Stuart and Joe Cannon, the man entrusted to mold the masked man's silver bullets. These deadly shootings take place in Chapter 11, but in the following one Morgan justifiably gets his from the business end of the Lone Ranger's six-shooters.

Leonard Clapham was born in 1889 and also first appeared in silents, his debut was in a 1915 Western, *Lone Larry*. After about ten years, he changed his name to Tom London. Among his credits was a role in *High Noon*, the 1952 Gary Cooper classic. *The Guinness Book of Movie Records* lists London as having made more film appearances than any other Hollywood performer. In December 1963, he passed away at 74.

In Chapter 13 of the serial, London's "trooper," Felton, is captured by the Lone Ranger and brought to the cave. He tangles with Dick Forrest and fails off a ledge to his death.

Perhaps John Merton's best moment in *The Lone Ranger* comes in Chapter 10 when he feels confident that the hero's identity will be revealed by the missing spur, only to be stunned when all of the Rangers have one missing. Throughout the serial, Merton's Kester is on a par with Stanley Andrews' gang leader, making for a formidable second-in-command with his jutting jaw and aggressive demeanor.

Merton assuredly proved a prolific player for Republic and directors Witney and English in a number of their serials. This also included roles in 1937's *Zorro Rides Again* and 1940's *Drums of Fu Manchu*. Born in 1901, John Merton was 58 when he died in September 1959.

The feature *Hi-Yo Silver*, made from the 1938 serial, gave top billing to Silver The Wonder Horse. The horse's actual name was Silver Chief, from the Hudkins Brothers Movie Ranch at Toluca Lake in California. The ranch was operated by Ace and Art Hudkins.

Lee Powell atop his Silver. Silver Chief was the horse's real name.

Silver Chief could be identified in its own Western film appearances by a unique cowlick of hair on its neck. Among the other cowboy stars who rode this famous horse at Republic were Robert Livingston in *The Lone Ranger Rides Again* and Sunset Carson in such adventures as 1946's *The El Paso Kid*. Carson initially called the horse Silver in his films, then began calling it Cactus. Another identifying mark for Silver Chief, seen in some Westerns but not the Lone Ranger adventures: dark spots near its right eye. In Charles Starrett's Durango Kid Westerns for Columbia, he also rode Silver Chief (he called the horse Raider). "Of all the 33 white horses I rode, here was the best," said Starrett.

My favorite Silver scene in *The Lone Ranger* is in the last chapter when the great steed breaks free and races after Rogers and King, who are on other mounts going for the ammo. Silver's nobility here was never better visualized.

Regarding the condensation of the *Lone Ranger* serial into the feature-length *Hi-Yo, Silver, Variety* reported in its April 17, 1940, review, "The only change, excepting the slashes, of course, is the insertion of intermittent scenes that show Raymond Hatton and an unbilled youngster [Dickie Jones] in scenes whose purpose is to narrate the flashback around which the major story unfolds."

An additional sequence not including Hatton or Jones was also in the feature (and later inserted into the DVD of the serial too). This is when President Abraham Lincoln sends Blanchard to Pecos, Texas. Lincoln was played by Frank McGlynn, Sr., an actor who originally played Lincoln on stage and then in a total of ten films. Among those other screen appearances were 1935's *The Littlest Rebel*, a Shirley Temple vehicle, and 1937's Joel McCrea Western *Wells Fargo*.

Hi-Yo, Silver opens at the Lazy Dude Ranch as Silver is being groomed by Smokey (Hatton), who tells the Lone Ranger tale to the boy (Jones). Later it is revealed that Hatton's old-timer is related to another youngster played by Sammy McKim in both serial and feature. Apparently McKim grew up to be Hatton's father so it is stretching things considerably to accept that Silver still looks young in this added portion. McKim appeared as a little Kit Carson in Republic's serial *The Painted Stallion*.

Father McKim, the supporting character played by William Farnum, is also part of the serial and feature. His carrier pigeons are used to send dire messages to the Lone Ranger. Farnum, born in 1876, was

In 1940, the 1938 *Lone Ranger* serial was edited to feature length and retitled *Hi-Yo Silver*.

a silent film star. In 1914's *The Spoilers*, he and Tom Santschi had one of the great movie fights, and they also coached Gary Cooper and William Boyd in the first sound remake in 1930 of that classic silent. At age 76 in 1953, Farnum passed away.

Many things from the serial were left out of the feature. For instance, Jim Clark's death is merely explained by Hatton to Jones. Also Dick Forrest's demise is said to have been caused by the fall off the cave ledge with Felton; therefore Kester's death, crushed beneath the falling stalactites, is gone too.

But foremost in both versions is the majestic camaraderie shared by the five brave and noble fighters for justice. Lee Powell, or perhaps Billy Bletcher, summed it up most eloquently after revealing his true identity: "You men have the spirit of Rangers," he said proudly.

For many years, the only available copies of the *Lone Ranger* serial had Spanish subtitles. Things have changed, however, thanks to the Internet and DVDs. Listed on Amazon com:lone rangers:movies & TV, I found DVDs of the serial and the condensed version. The latter is of better quality, but each one is very enjoyable and with no subtitles.

The serial is part of a four-disc set called *Gun Justice—Featuring the Lone Ranger*. Also included are 17 episodes from the TV series and even TV episodes from early Westerns like *The Cisco Kid* and *The Roy Rogers Show*. *Hi-Yo Silver* is part of another DVD called *The Lone Ranger Classic Western Double Feature*. Also part of this set: the first three episodes of the TV series under the title *Legend of the Lone Ranger*.

Four

The 1939 Serial
The Lone Ranger Rides Again

The Lone Ranger has the respect
of all law-abiding people. He stands for justice.
—Judge Miller to Craig Dolan, who objects to the presence
of the Masked Man in a courtroom

Released by Republic on February 25, 1939. 15 chapters; 263 minutes; black and white. Based on a story by Gerald Geraghty, and characters created by George W. Trendle and Fran Striker.

Credits:
Directors: William Witney, John English.
Producer: Robert Beche.
Screenplay: Franklin Adreon, Ronald Davidson, Sol Shor, Barry Shipman.
Photography: William Nobles, Edgar Lyons.
Editors: Helene Turner, Edward Todd.
Art Directors: John Victor Mackay, Ralph Oberg.
Set Decorator: Morris Braun.
Costumes: Robert Ramsey, Adele Palmer.
Special Effects: Howard Lydecker, Theodore Lydecker.
Musical Directors: William Lava, Cy Feur.

Cast:
Robert Livingston (Bill Andrews/The Lone Ranger); Chief Thundercloud (Tonto); Duncan Renaldo (Juan Vasquez); Jinx Falken (Sue Dolan); Ralph Dunn (Bart Dolan); J. Farrell MacDonald (Craig Dolan); William Gould (Jed Scott); Rex Lease (Evans); Theodore Mapes (Merritt); Henry Otho (Pa Daniels); John Beach (Hardin); Glenn Strange (Thorne); Stanley Blystone (Murdock); Edwin Parker (Hank); Al Taylor (Colt); Carleton Young (Logan); Betty Roadman (Ma Daniels); Ernie Adams (Doc Grover); Forrest Taylor (Judge Miller); Buddy Roo-

sevelt (Slade); Charles Whitaker (Black); Rob Robinson (Blackie); Ralph LeFever (Bill); Bob McClung (Danny Daniels); Roger Williams (Sheriff); Howard Chase (Gibson); Buddy Messenger (Rance); Joe Perez (Diego Vasquez); Silver Chief (Silver).

CHAPTER 1 "The Lone Ranger Returns," 28 minutes, 54 seconds: In New Mexico, Juan Vasquez rides onto the family ranchero to find the place burning and brother Diego mortally wounded. Before he dies, Diego says he was shot by the Lone Ranger. Catching up to the Lone Ranger, Juan is soon overpowered in their struggle. The Ranger denies doing the shooting and asks Juan for a few days to clear his name and find the imposter who actually did it. On the trail, the Ranger and Juan are joined by Tonto, the former's companion. The Ranger reveals the trouble between the ranchers and homesteaders. After Tonto and the Lone Ranger ride on, Juan helps Jed Scott, the leader of the homestead-

Robert Livingston and Duncan Renaldo find the Lone Ranger imposter, played by Carleton Young, in this scene from 1939's *The Lone Ranger Rides Again*.

ers, against some troublemakers. One troublemaker works for cattleman Craig Dolan. Although he opposes the homesteaders over water rights, Dolan claims the troublemaker is a man he fired. In the town of San Ramon, Jed Scott is put on trial for the murder of Doc Grover. However, the Lone Ranger wants to help Jed. Juan and a man sympathetic to the homesteaders, Bill Andrews, chase an impostor Lone Ranger and Juan shoots him. It's really a man named Logan, who while dying says that Grover was shot by another man, Slade. Andrews reveals to Juan that he is the real Lone Ranger. The Ranger learns that the Grover killing was a fake. In town, gunmen secretly working for Craig Dolan's nephew Bart get in a gunfight with homesteaders. When a bullet strikes a lighted lamp in the jailhouse, it starts a fire which threatens the life of Jed, locked in a cell. The Lone Ranger rushes in to Jed just as the roof collapses.

CHAPTER 2 "Masked Victory," 16 minutes, 43 seconds: A rope is tied by Juan to Silver, the Ranger's horse, and to the bars on the jailhouse window. When the bars are pulled out, the Masked Man and Jed escape. When Jed is put on trial for Doc Grover's murder, the Lone Ranger claims it is a frame-up and that Grover is alive. Tonto, sent to bring in Grover and Slade, is captured by Dolan's men. Everyone from the courthouse prepares to visit the alleged grave of Grover to see whether he is dead or not. To produce a body for the court, some of Dolan's men actually plan on killing Grover. The Lone Ranger arrives in time to save Grover and free Tonto. Meantime, Bart Dolan creates mob frenzy to get Jed lynched. The Ranger saves the day only to be shot from his horse by Slade.

CHAPTER 3 "The Black Raiders Strike," 16 minutes, 45 seconds: When the Lone Ranger falls from his horse after being shot, Juan shoots down Slade. A bag of silver carried by the Ranger stopped the bullet. Jed Scott tells Craig Dolan that the law gives the homesteaders water rights. Dolan warns then about the Black Raiders, vigilantes who prey on homesteaders. The Ranger, Tonto and Juan see Bart Dolan meet with the Raiders. The Ranger trails the Raiders, while his companions follow Bart, who is on a horse with a broken shoe. Aware of this, Bart exchanges his horse with his sister Sue's mount to get away. Sue is not aware of her brother's deception. When the Ranger comes under attack from the Raiders, Sue helps him escape. Learning that the Black Raiders are after homesteader Pa Daniels and his family, the Ranger sends Sue to alert Jed Scott while he rides to the Daniels' defense. Jed and Juan feel Sue may be trying to trick them and so the Ranger must help the family alone. Able to help them get away, the Lone Ranger is then stuck in deep mud attempting a river crossing on foot.

CHAPTER 4   "The Cavern of Doom," 16 minutes, 44 seconds: Using a rope, Tonto pulls the Lone Ranger free of the mud. The Ranger then chases after the Raiders to retrieve Pa Daniels' stolen supply wagon. Bart Dolan realizes that his sister is following him and pretends to be a prisoner of the Raiders. The ruse fools Sue, Tonto and the Ranger when they ride to Dolan's rescue as he is tied up in a cave. The Black Raiders and Bart slip away leaving their two adversaries trapped behind a large gate. A powderkeg is lit before the Raiders ride out, and the Lone Ranger and Tonto struggle to put out the fuse. But an explosion is soon heard.

CHAPTER 5   "Agents of Deceit," 16 minutes, 37 seconds: Prior to the explosion, the Ranger gets Silver to push the lit powderkeg aside way and then has the horse pull down the gate. When the explosion is heard, Bart and the Raiders think their adversaries are killed. As Sue is threatened by the Raiders, the Ranger goes to the aid of her and Bart; neither she nor the Ranger are aware of Dolan's duplicity. Neither is Craig Dolan, who plans on fighting the homesteaders with legal means over the water rights. When the homesteaders receive a wagon of seed for their crops, Bart sends Raiders to destroy it. The Raiders send a burning wagon down a hillside toward the seed wagon. Jumping onto the burning wagon is the Lone Ranger.

CHAPTER 6   "The Trap," 16 minutes, 39 seconds: Diverting the burning wagon, the Ranger leaps to safety. The Black Raiders want to steal land claim forms, locked in the jailhouse safe. The sheriff rigs the safe with a gun. Two of Bart's henchmen, Blackie and Rance, threaten a clerk to get the safe's combination. Helping the clerk are Tonto and Juan. Having overheard the combination number, the Ranger races to the jailhouse and dials the combination. The blast from the rigged gun is heard.

CHAPTER 7   "Lone Ranger at Bay," 16 minutes, 42 seconds: The fired bullet hits a Black Raider, not the Ranger. The Lone Ranger takes the land claim forms. Craig Dolan insists that the sheriff and a posse retrieve the forms, and Bart offers a reward to have the Ranger killed. Juan and Bill Andrews feign a fight to give Jed Scott time to hide the claim forms. Working with the homesteaders to then get the forms out of town are Andrews and Vasquez. Pursuing them is the sheriff's posse. The Lone Ranger is trapped in a shack as posse members inadvertently start a landslide above it.

CHAPTER 8 "Ambush," 16 minutes, 40 seconds: With rocks crashing down, the Lone Ranger makes a last-second escape on Silver. The sheriff is killed by the falling rocks. With a new sheriff needed, Pa Daniels is nominated by the homesteaders. Deputy Joe Parker is nominated by the cattlemen. To discourage Daniels from running, Black Raiders kidnap his son Danny. When Pa goes to help him, he too is taken captive. The Ranger rides to the cave where the captives are held and rescues them. Just outside the cave waiting to ambush them is one of the Raiders.

Robert Livingston primed for action in *The Lone Ranger Rides Again*.

CHAPTER 9 "Wheels of Doom," 16 minutes, 44 seconds: Leaving the cave, Pa Daniels is wounded by the Raider. As he is now unable to run for sheriff due to the injury, Jed Scott is nominated instead. When Bart Dolan learns of the new nomination, he has his Raiders attack Scott, the Ranger and Tonto. Tonto and the Masked Man catch their foes in a crossfire, forcing them to flee. After the election for sheriff, the ballot box of votes is locked up for the night to be counted the next morning. Bart, intending to change votes if needed, has them stolen and placed in a passing wagon. The Ranger and a Raider fight aboard the wagon as it careens down a steep hillside.

CHAPTER 10 "The Dangerous Captive," 16 minutes, 37 seconds: Before the wagon crashes, the Ranger jumps clear. The ballots, returned to town, are counted and Jed is the new sheriff. Among his appointed deputies are Juan and Andrews. Bart arranges for one of the Raiders, Lynch, to rustle his (Bart's) uncle's cattle. It is a ruse to lure the deputies

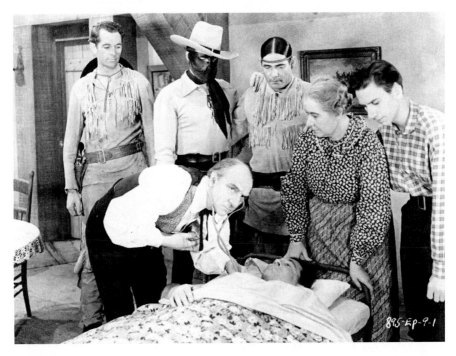

Surrounded by fellow cast members in the 1939 serial are Robert Livingston's Masked Man and Chief Thundercloud's Tonto.

into a trap. While attempting to warn them, Tonto is taken by the Black Raiders. The Lone Ranger rescues Tonto and takes Lynch to jail.

To keep Lynch from informing on Bart, the Raiders place a burning powderkeg outside the jailhouse. Andrews and Vasquez try to stop them. Bill is atop the jailhouse with the lit fuse burning shorter.

CHAPTER 11 "Death Below," 16 minutes, 40 seconds: With a rope, Andrews pulls the lit powderkeg away and it then blows up near some of the Raiders. Gibson, the Federal Land Registrar assigned to handle the between the cattlemen-homesteaders dispute, is waylaid by Bart's men and taken to their hideout. The Lone Ranger rescues Gibson and both men attempt to fight off the Black Raiders. High atop a rock formation, Tonto lowers a rope for the two to climb to safety. While Gibson reaches safety, the rope breaks as the Ranger attempts to climb.

CHAPTER 12 "Blazing Peril," 16 minutes, 41 seconds: The Ranger falls into some bushes uninjured. The broken rope is thrown to Tonto, who secures it for the Ranger to escape from the Raiders. Despite his ordeal, Gibson is determined to hear both sides of the land dispute. First he listens to the homesteaders who have gathered at a neighboring barn. As previous events are being discussed, Black Raiders secretly set it on fire. Everyone inside seems to be trapped, including Bill Andrews.

CHAPTER 13 "Exposed," 16 minutes, 42 seconds: Everyone in the burning barn escapes through a trapdoor. Believing they are dead, the Raiders ride off. While Gibson feels that Craig Dolan is behind the Black Raiders, Andrews is unsure. Craig discovers that his nephew is indeed leader of the Raiders, and Bart shoots him. Sue is held at gunpoint by her brother to force Juan, Tonto and the Lone Ranger to drop their guns. Bart then locks them in a room and tries to escape. Craig, the Ranger and Tonto follow Bart to his hideout in an abandoned mine cave. When Bart sends a mine cart racing down a track at the Masked Man, he outruns it until he comes to a dead end.

CHAPTER 14 "Besieged," 16 minutes, 39 seconds: The mine cart is derailed when the Lone Ranger blocks the track. Some of the Black Raiders are reluctant to face the threat of the Federal Cavalry, so Bart rounds up still more outlaws in an all-out war against the homesteaders. The Evans farm is the first attacked by Dolan's army. Helping the family are Scott's deputies, including Evans and Bill Andrews. All the homesteaders are being alerted to seek refuge in an old fort. When Bart's army reaches the fort, Andrews tries to divert the enemy and is chased down.

CHAPTER 15 "Frontier Justice," 16 minutes, 45 seconds: As Bill is shot at by Dolan's men, he feigns being hurt by falling off his horse. Thinking he is dead, the men ride away. Andrews then becomes the Lone Ranger and rides for the cavalry. The Ranger is soon leading the troops to the fort, which is under attack by Dolan's men. When Bart thinks a lit powderkeg has been defused by the Ranger in a wagon pushed to the fort's gate by his men, he enters it only to be blown to smithereens.

The cavalrymen round up the rest of Bart's gang. Jed Scott and Craig Dolan agree to a peaceful co-existence. Joining Tonto and the Lone Ranger when they ride off together is Juan Vasquez.

La Vuelta del Llanero Solitario is the Spanish title for *The Lone Ranger Rides Again*. The two-disc DVD set I found on Amazon includes this Spanish subtitles. But the cast and credit names are all in English, as are the speaking voices.

This particular DVD version, however, did delete the chapter titles, making the showing appear to be a lengthy film rather than a serial. I do understand that other DVD producers have returned to the original serial format and with a better quality print than the one I experienced.

Like the 1938 *Lone Ranger* serial, *Rides Again* utilized Iverson Ranch locations. Other California locations for *Rides Again* included Bronson Canyon and Kernville. It was filmed under the title *The Lone Ranger Returns* between December 9, 1938, and January 20, 1939.

The serial's production costs of $213,997 made it the studio's most expensive one for 1939. Apparently it was not the success the first one was. William Witney, back as co-director with John English, believed the script was not as good as the original adventure. Nonetheless, there were plenty of shootouts, horse chases and fistfights. Writers Barry Shipman, Ronald Davidson and Franklin Adreon were again on board, joined by Gerald Geraghty and Sol Shor.

Yakima Canutt was back doing magnificent stunt work doubling for our masked hero. He was ably assisted by George DeNormand, who performed one or two really neat backflips in the guise of the Ranger.

DeNormand, born in 1903, was 73 when he passed away in December 1976. As an actor, he appeared in many films and TV shows over the years. Along with being a posseman in *The Lone Ranger Rides Again*, DeNormand was also in Republic's most expensive serial, *Captain America*, in 1944. His initial television work was in several 1950 episodes of Duncan Renaldo's *Cisco Kid* series.

Ken Cooper was not around to help out with the stunts in the second serial. He did double its star, Bob Livingston, in at least two earlier Westerns, 1937's *Riders of the Whistling Skull* and 1936's *Roarin' Lead*. Born Virgil Kenneth Cooper in 1896, he was a trick rider in the very first Western to win the Academy Award for Best Picture, 1931's *Cimarron*. He died at 92 in March 1989.

Robert Livingston's Bill Andrews was revealed early in the second serial as the Lone Ranger, but only to Duncan Renaldo's Juan Vasquez. Tonto, of course, knew the Ranger's identity even before the new story unfolded. Unlike the 1938's *The Lone Ranger*, only two other characters know the secret.

Apparently Lee Powell wanted to return as Allen King, but Republic's second scenario called for an entirely new character. Silver Chief returned as the Masked Man's beloved steed. Reportedly Silver Chief was the horse rode by Thomas Mitchell in the Best Picture Oscar winner of 1939, *Gone with the Wind*.

Billy Bletcher once again was the voice for the Lone Ranger. Although equally commanding, he was not as loud as he was in his initial turn except perhaps for his "Hi-Yo, Silver!"s.

Tonto's horse Scout was played by Sunny and actually owned by Chief Thundercloud (real name: Victor Daniels). The actor also used the steed in other films, along with another horse he owned called Smoke. Both horses appeared in a 1936 Dick Foran Western, *California Mail*.

On the August 5, 1938, episode of the Lone Ranger radio show, "Four-Day Ride," Tonto was first given the horse Scout as a gift. The steed replaced another called White Feller. However, Tonto did not actually refer to his new horse as Scout until the radio episode on September 2, 1938, "Border Dope Smuggling." Tonto initially referred to Scout as his "paint horse" only.

From 1936 to 1941, Bob Livingston portrayed Stoney Brooke, one of the Three Mesquiteers, in 29 Republic "B" Westerns. In one 1939 entry, *Kansas Terrors*, he also appeared in the Lone Ranger costume. Most likely it was a plug for the new serial.

In Livingston's first starring role in a Western, 1936's *The Bold Caballero*, he portrayed another famous dual role, Don Diego and Zorro. With both a dashing and charming screen persona, the actor certainly was a fitting choice as Bill Andrews and the Lone Ranger.

In Livingston's scenes with Duncan Renaldo, likewise a very personable performer, there's a real chemistry between the two. And nowhere more than in Chapter 7 with their amusing feigned fistfight. They also appeared together in several of the Three Mesquiteers adventures, including 1940's *Heroes of the Saddle*, directed by the serial's William Witney.

After his days riding the range on the big screen, Livingston appeared on television in Renaldo's *The Cisco Kid* and Clayton Moore's *The Lone Ranger* (he was in the episodes "Frame for Two" [1952] and "Message to Fort Apache" [1954] of the latter). Born in 1908 as Robert Randall (his brother Jack Randall was a "B" Western star in the 1930s), Livingston passed away in 1988 at the age of 79.

Duncan Renaldo first played writer O. Henry's Western hero "The Cisco Kid" in a 1945 film, *The Cisco Kid Returns*, and proceeded to play the role in other films and on television. When production closed on the TV series *The Cisco Kid* in 1955, Renaldo and Leo Carrillo (who played his sidekick Pancho) entertained viewers for years afterwards in reruns.

Renaldo's initial outing as a Mesquiteer with Bob Livingston was *Kansas Terrors* and his last in 1940 was *Oklahoma Renegades*. His Vasquez in the second Lone Ranger serial proved an able ally for the Masked Man and Tonto.

Born in 1904 in either in Spain or New Jersey (sources differ), Renaldo's colorful, dynamic personality was always a plus and especially so as Cisco. Like Clayton Moore, he enjoyed making personal appearances as one of TV's most memorable characters. In 1980, he died from an apparent heart attack when he was 76.

Eugenia Lincoln Falkenburg was born in 1919. Nicknamed Jinx, she became one of America's first supermodels, gracing more than 200 magazine covers in the 1930s and 1940s. She was also an avid tennis player; her younger brother Bob was a Wimbledon champion in 1948. Billed as Jinx Falken in *Lone Ranger Rides Again*, she gives a convincing performance as Sue Dolan, the feisty beauty. caught in the middle of the difficulties with her uncle, brother and the homesteaders. Especially relevant were her spirited moments in Chapter 3 when she helps the Lone Ranger get away from the Black Raiders and then tries to warn Jed Scott of their menace.

Jinx and her husband, Tex McCrary, began a radio show, *Hi Jinx*, in 1946. They interviewed popular entertainers and public figures; other shows with various titles followed both on radio and television. She retired from her regular duties in broadcasting around 1958. In June 2003, Jinx passed away at age 84.

Portraying Craig Dolan was longtime character actor J. Farrell MacDonald. Born in 1875 with the first name of Joseph, he started his career making short silent films in 1911. He taught acting in the mid–1930s at the University of California. The stern yet vulnerable persona MacDonald projected in *Lone Ranger Rides Again* was put to good use in other films as well. One of his truly great moments in films, as Mac the barman for John Ford's *My Darling Clementine* in 1946, still makes me smile: When asked by Henry Fonda's Wyatt Earp if he has ever been in love, Mac replies, "No, I been a bartender all me life." That same year, MacDonald appeared as the curmudgeon who owns the tree James Stewart crashes into in *It's a Wonderful Life*. In August 1952, the actor passed on at age 77.

MacDonald's counterpart in the serial was William Gould as Jed Scott. Scott bore a slight resemblance to the first Ranger serial's Stanley Andrews. William Howard Gould was born in 1886 and died in May 1969. During the 1930s, he was also seen as the heavy in Westerns and appeared with "B" cowboy stars Ken Maynard and Tom Tyler. In 1960, he was in the Alan Ladd Western *Guns of the Timberland*. Stand-out moments for Gould in the Ranger serial included being wrongly accused of murder in Chapter 2 and elected sheriff in Chapter 10.

Henry Otho plays Paul Daniels in *Rides Again*. His best moments are in Chapter 8, when he is the initial nominee for sheriff, and in Chapter 9 when he is injured by a Black Raider. Born in 1888 as Henry Otho Wright, his film career was a relatively short one beginning in 1931 and ending with his death in June 1940. In 1939, Otho was in Errol Flynn's first Western, *Dodge City*.

Our masked hero appears to be on the wrong side of the law in Chapter 1 of *The Lone Ranger Rides Again.* Impersonating the Ranger, in a small but impressive role, was Carleton Young. Born Carleton Scott Young in 1905, he died at age 89 in 1994. Busy at Republic early in his career, he participated in their *Dick Tracy* serial in 1937 as the crime-fighter's brother. Young had a great moment in the John Ford Western *The Man Who Shot Liberty Valance* (1962): After James Stewart's Ranse Stoddard tells the true story, Young's newspaperman replies, "This is the West, Sir. When the legend becomes fact, print the legend."

As Doc Grover, Ernie Adams (1885–1947) conveyed the shifty, weasel-like characteristics needed. In Chapter 2, he is more than a little surprised when the tables are turned on him after trying to frame Jed Scott for his own "murder." Only because he faces annihilation by his fellow Black Raiders does Grover untie a captive Tonto. Adams had many "B" Westerns to his credit and a fine selection of "A" films as well. At least two of the latter were with Gary Cooper: 1929's *The Virginian* and 1942's *The Pride of the Yankees*, where he played manager Miller Huggins.

Playing Slade, one of the gang leaders early in the serial, was Buddy Roosevelt. Attempting to kill the Lone Ranger for exposing him as the mastermind of the Scott frame-up, this particularly unsavory Black Raider gets his comeuppance in Chapter 3 from Juan. Roosevelt's film career began in the silent era doubling for early Western star William S. Hart. He appeared in another Republic film in 1939, *Man of Conquest*, as one of the Alamo defenders. Born in 1898 as Kenneth Stanhope Sanderson, he passed away at 75 in 1973.

Lew Meehan played another Black Raider, Lynch, ordered by head honcho Bart Dolan to rustle cattle in Chapter 10. Born James Lew Meehan in 1890, he died in 1951 at 60.

Seen unbilled as one of the heavies, involved in the serial's cave fight between the Lone Ranger, Tonto and the Black Raiders, was Dave Sharpe. While Yakima Canutt was called the King of the Stuntmen, Sharpe was deemed the Crown Prince. He became Republic's stunt coordinator in 1939 and served with great distinction until 1942 when he left for World War II service.

David Hardin Sharpe, born in 1910, later doubled for Clayton Moore's TV Lone Ranger in a 1954 episode called "The Globe." In at least five films, including 1958's *The Vikings*, Sharpe doubled for Tony

Curtis. It was Curtis who gave the eulogy at Sharpe's funeral. He was 70 when he died in 1980.

A true Westerner, George Glenn Strange was born in New Mexico in 1899. Early in his lifetime, he was both a deputy sheriff and rancher. He began his movie career in the early 1930s as an extra and bit player. He was one of the drovers with John Wayne in 1948's *Red River*.

Given a prominent role as Thorne in the 1939 serial, Strange seemed like the leader of the Black Raiders. Among his dastardly deeds was the Chapter 8 kidnapping of young Danny Daniels (Robert McClung), to dissuade the boy's father from running for sheriff. Thorne is rounded up with the remaining Raiders in the last chapter.

This was ten years before Strange's first villainous stint as Butch Cavendish on the *Lone Ranger* series. And more than 20 years before he began the recurring role of Sam the bartender in the *Gunsmoke* series. After a dozen years on *Gunsmoke*, Strange died of lung cancer in September 1973. He was 76 years old.

There was a tendency to initially believe that cattleman Craig Dolan (J. Farrell MacDonald) formed the Black Raiders, due to his formidable opposition to the homesteaders. While nephew Bart's hand in things is revealed earlier to viewers, it is not until Chapter 13 that his uncle discovers the truth. Ralph Dunn's playing of the contemptible Bart was more thug than gang leader, thus lacking the intensity the role demanded. However, another part of the problem might be due to sharing the leadership with the strong characters played by Mac-Donald, Glenn Strange and Buddy Roosevelt.

Born in 1900, Dunn began his movie career in 1932's *The Crowd Roars*, one of James Cagney's early films. With his big burly frame and a bullying presence, the actor seemed a perfect foil when he appeared with the Three Stooges in their comedy shorts *Mummy's Dummies* (1948) and *Who Done It?* (1949). At age 67, he passed away in 1968.

In *The Encyclopedia of Western Movies*, Phil Hardy compared *Rides Again* to the first serial and called it "a routine outing." The online *Files of Jerry Blake* called it "the weakest of Republic's Golden Age serials." Both criticisms had some validity. Despite directors John English and William Witney having more control this time over casting, a few choices seemed glaring enough to weaken the serial's potential, as already related. Somewhat glaring too was the lack of clarity over whether the original San Ramon sheriff (Roger Williams) was a good or bad guy.

Yet the incredible action sequences were every bit as good as those in the first serial, thanks to the direction and to the exceptional editing of Helene Turner and Edward Todd. One of my favorite action highlights occurred in Chapter 13, with the Lone Ranger racing along a mine tunnel track to escape the out-of-control cart bearing down on him.

Another plus was William Lava's music direction. While Rossini's *William Tell Overture* was once more the pivotal music heard, von Suppe's *Light Cavalry Overture* is heard in Chapter 3 and then showcased in the exciting if clichéd sequence in Chapter 15 when the Ranger leads the troops to the rescue of the homesteaders.

Duncan Renaldo's sidekick Juan never overshadows Chief Thundercloud's heroics. Particularly exciting in this regard was Tonto's shooting Bart Dolan's gun right out of his hand in Chapter 13 to save the Ranger's life.

Robert Livingston's contribution to the Lone Ranger legend had to be a source of pride for him. Years later when the TV series was being cast, he tried unsuccessfully to win the starring role.

Silver and Scout enhanced their legendary status over the course of *The Lone Ranger Rides Again*. In Chapter 5, the Masked Man and Tonto need but whistle and the horses are at their side to help them escape from the powderkeg explosion.

The Clayton Moore TV series featured more of the great Lone Ranger-Tonto adventures, immortalizing fully the legend of the Lone Ranger.

Five

The 1949–1957 TV Series
The Lone Ranger

Mr. Trendle, I am the Lone Ranger!
—Clayton Moore to George W. Trendle
during their 1949 meeting

Original 30-minute broadcasts on ABC-TV (September 1949–September 1957); Thursdays, 7:30–8:00 p.m.; 221 episodes. From The Lone Ranger, Inc./George W. Trendle and Apex Film Corp./Jack Chertok, 1949–54; Jack Wrather Productions/Jack Wrather, 1954–57.

Credits:
Producers: Sherman A. Harris, Paul Landers.
Executive Producer: Harry Poppe.
Directors: George Archainbaud (1949–50); George B. Seitz, Jr. (1949–51); John H. Morse (1950–53); Paul Landres (1952–53); William Thiele (1954–55); Oscar Rudolph (1954–57); Charles D. Livingstone (1955); Earl Bellamy (1956–57).
Writers: Andre Lamb (1949); Gibson Fox, Polly James, Doris Schroeder (1949–50); George B. Seitz, Jr. (1949–53); Harry Poppe, Jr. (1949–55); Fran Striker (1949–56); Edmond Kelso, Tom Seller, George W. Trendle (1949–57); David Bramson, Eve Greene David Lang, Sherman L. Lowe, Joseph F. Poland, Milton Ralson, Louise Rousseau, Francis P. Scannell (1950); Herb Meadow (1950–51); David P. Sheppard (1950–53); Don Beattie, Ralph Goll, Felix Holt, Betty Joyce, Curtis Kenyon, Joe Richardson (1950–55). Marjorie Fortin (1951); Tom Dougall (1951–55); Charles Larson (1952–57); Robert Halff, Terence Maples, John Thiele (1953); William Bruckner, Steve McCarthy (1953–55); Oscar Larson, Elwood Ullman (1954); Jack Laird, Bert Lambert (1954–55); Eric Freiwald, Robert Schaefer (1954–57); Lee Berg, Albert Duffy, Frank L. Moss, Samuel Rice, Lillian Rose, George Van Marter (1955); Melvin Levy, Jack

Natteford, Walter A. Tompkins (1956); Robert Leslie Bellem, Doane R. Hoag, Hilary Crestan Rhodes, Wells Root (1956–57); Orville H. Hampton, Herbert Purdom, DeVallon Scott (1957); also Dwight V. Babcock, Hal G. Evarts.

Editors: Richard G. Wray (1949–52); Axel Hubert, Sr. (1949–53); Ben Marmon (1949–55); Frank Capacchione, Everett Dodd (1949–57); Marsh Hendry (1950–55); Byron Chudnow, Ernie Leadlay, Harvey Manger (1953); Stanley Rabjohn (1954–55); Elma Veron (1955); Hal Gordon (1956); also John Faure, Stanley Frazen.

Directors of Photography: Mack Stengler (1949–51); Robert Pittack (1952–55); William P. Whitley (1956–57).

Cast:
Clayton Moore as the Lone Ranger (1949–52, 1954–57); John Hart as the Lone Ranger (1952–54); Jay Silverheels as Tonto (1949–57).

First Season (52 Episodes; Black and White)

1 "Enter the Lone Ranger" (9/15/49). Clayton Moore, Jay Silverheels, Jack Clifford, Tristram Coffin, George Lewis, Glenn Strange. Six Texas Rangers are ambushed by Butch Cavendish's gang of outlaws and left for dead. One Ranger, found alive by the Indian Tonto, recovers.

2 "The Lone Ranger Fights On" (9/22/49). Clayton Moore, Jay Silverheels, George Chesebro, George Lewis, Ralph Littlefield, Walter Sande, Glenn Strange. The Lone Ranger and Tonto go after Collins, the guide who betrayed the Texas Rangers to the Cavendish gang. Then the Ranger secures the silver bullets needed and the stallion Silver.

3 "The Lone Ranger's Triumph" (9/29/49). Clayton Moore, Jay Silverheels, George Chesebro, Jack Clifford, Walter Sande, Glenn Strange. Proving a helpful ally with Tonto and the Lone Ranger is Sheriff Two-Gun Taylor. Soon Butch Cavendish and his cohorts are brought to justice.

4 "The Legion of Old Timers" (10/6/49). Clayton Moore, Jay Silverheels, Lane Bradford, DeForest Kelley, Emmett Lynn, Norman Willis. A tenderfoot inherits a ranch and is in danger of losing it to outlaws. The Ranger and Tonto save the day with the help of the elderly ranch hands.

The most famous Lone Ranger of all, Clayton Moore, with his own Silver.

5 "Rustler's Hideout" (10/13/49). Clayton Moore, Jay Silverheels, Joseph Crehan, Dickie Jones, Harry Lauter, Kay Morley. After ranchers capture outlaw Pete Madden, his gang kidnap a rancher's son. The Lone Ranger infiltrates the gang to rescue the boy.

6 "War Horse" (10/20/49). Clayton Moore, Jay Silverheels, Jean DeBriac, John Merton, Leonard Penn, Chief Yowlachie. Hunter Madrigo plots the theft of a chief's war horse. The Ranger and Tonto must contend with a possible Indian war breaking out.

7 "Pete and Pedro" (10/27/49). Clayton Moore, Jay Silverheels, Rufe Davis, Don Diamond, John Parrish, Sheila Ryan. A cattleman tries to force a young lady to sell her ranch. A pair of bickering cowpokes assist Tonto and the Ranger on her behalf.

8 "The Renegades" (11/3/49). Clayton Moore, Jay Silverheels, Lane Chandler, Harry Harvey, Kenneth MacDonald, Ralph Moody, Gene Roth. Army deserters and an Indian agent are up to no good. The Lone Ranger must stop them from killing Tonto and his old friend Chief Swift Eagle.

9 "The Tenderfeet" (11/10/49). Clayton Moore, Jay Silverheels, Ray Bennett, Rand Brooks, Ross Ford, Hank Worden. Discovering a valuable claim, the Larabee brothers are framed for claim-jumping and murder. It is up to the Lone Ranger to help them.

10 "High Heels" (11/17/49). Clayton Moore, Jay Silverheels, Stanley Andrews, Johnny Berkes, Earle Hodgins, James Sheldon. Pat St. Ives is sensitive about being short. When Monk Gow makes trouble, Tonto and the Ranger show that height does not prove a man's worth.

11 "Six-Gun Legacy" (11/24/49). Clayton Moore, Jay Silverheels, Don Haggerty, James J. Hickman, Hal Price, Ian Wolfe. To keep him from an inheritance, outlaws plan on having Bob Walker impersonated. Learning that Bob has been hurt by the outlaws, the Ranger and Tonto go after them.

12 "The Return of the Convict" (12/1/49). Clayton Moore, Jay Silverheels, Steve Clark, John Day, Robert Emmett Keane, John Kellogg. After being falsely imprisoned, John Amos tries to find out the truth and is almost lynched. He is helped by the Lone Ranger and Tonto.

13 "Finders Keepers" (12/8/49). Clayton Moore, Jay Silverheels, Pedro de Cordova, Arthur Franz, Francis MacDonald, Carol Thurston. Blackmailed into robbing a bank, Nat Parker is imprisoned. Freed, Nat and the Lone Ranger recover the stolen money.

14 "The Masked Rider" (12/15/49). Clayton Moore, Jay Silverheels, John Alvin, John Doucette, Nan Leslie, Ed Rand. An imposter calling himself the Lone Ranger is committing crimes. The real Ranger must clear his own name.

15 "Old Joe's Sister" (12/22/49). Clayton Moore, Jay Silverheels, Wade Crosby, Joel Friedkin, Anne O'Neal, Lester Sharpe. Waiting to see a long-lost sister, Old Joe is attacked by a couple of outlaws. The Lone Ranger and Joe's sister come to his aid.

16 "Cannonball McKay" (12/29/49). Clayton Moore, Jay Silverheels, Tristram Coffin, Louise Lorimer, Charles Meredith, Leonard Strong. Two no-goods try to kill Clem Jones after framing him for robbery. But lady stagecoach driver Cannonball McKay and the Lone Ranger are there to help him.

17 "The Man Who Came Back" (1/5/50). Clayton Moore, Jay Silverheels, Robert Carson, Roy Gordon, Martha Hyer, Emmett Lynn, Robert J. Wilke. Tonto and the Ranger discover their friend Joe Crawford is missing from his ranch. A man named Gavin is trying to cheat Joe out of it.

18 "Outlaw Town" (1/12/50). Clayton Moore, Jay Silverheels, Marshall Bradford, John Eldredge, Greta Granstedt, Gene Reynolds. · Outlaw Town, a place for criminals to hide out, is run by Jack Burke. His wife can only take so much and turns to the Lone Ranger.

19 "Greed for Gold" (1/19/50). Clayton Moore, Jay Silverheels, Lane Bradford, Kenne Duncan, Kermit Maynard, Duke York. The Ranger and Tonto find an old friend has been killed. Discovering that a gold mine is involved helps them unmask the killer.

20 "Man of the House" (1/26/50). Clayton Moore, Jay Silverheels, Lane Chandler, Stanley Farrar, Tim Graham, Esther Somers. A timid man, Casper, is bullied at home by his wife. Spending time with Tonto and the Lone Ranger chasing outlaws gives the man the strength to stand up to her.

21 "Barnaby Boggs, Esquire" (2/2/50). Clayton Moore, Jay Silverheels, Holly Bane, Bill Kennedy, Hal Price, Gene Roth. Kruger has been able to keep his outlaw activities a secret from the townsfolk. Things change when Barnaby Boggs, the Lone Ranger's friend, arrives.

22 "Sheep Thieves" (2/9/50). Clayton Moore, Jay Silverheels, Russ Conway, Chuck Courtney, Pedro de Cordova, Jimmy Ogg. Dan Reid, the Lone Ranger's nephew, pretends to be a rancher's grandson. The ruse to catch rustlers results in Dan being held for ransom.

23 "Jim Tyler's Past" (2/16/50). Clayton Moore, Jay Silverheels, Ray Bennett, Rand Brooks, Peter Mamakos, House Peters, Jr. Jim Tyler is harboring a secret discovered by Tonto and the Lone Ranger. It may affect Tyler's future as a lawman.

24 "The Man with Two Faces" (2/23/50). Clayton Moore, Jay Silverheels, Stanley Andrews, Chris Drake, Earle Hodgins, Mira McKinney. Robberies are committed at three of Joshua Blaine's banks. Tonto and the Ranger get involved when one of Blaine's nephews is accused.

25 "Buried Treasure" (3/2/50). Clayton Moore, Jay Silverheels, David Bruce, William Challee, Gail Davis, William Gould. Roy Foster and his wife are forced to deal with an escaped convict (Roy's brother). The Ranger and Tonto find a way to help the couple.

26 "Troubled Waters" (3/9/50). Clayton Moore, Jay Silverheels, Dick Alexander, Billy Bletcher, Byron Foulger, Harry Lauter. The Ranger helps Dave Tucker contend with another person over the oil found on his ranch.

27 "Gold Train" (3/16/50). Clayton Moore, Jay Silverheels, Erville Alderson, Billy Bletcher, Frank Fenton, DeForest Kelley. Mistakenly identified as the Dude, a masked outlaw, the Lone Ranger is put behind bars. He escapes to clear his name.

28 "Pay Dirt" (3/23/50). Clayton Moore, Jay Silverheels, George Lewis, Emmett Lynn, Martin Milner, Zon Murray, Walter Sande. Claim jumpers are ready to resort to murder to get their way. But Tonto and the Ranger are more than a match for them.

29 "Billie the Great" (3/30/50). Clayton Moore, Jay Silverheels, Ward Blackburn, Steve Clark, James Flavin, Minerva Urecal. Lady barber Billie safeguards the town's money. Helping to keep outlaws away from it is the Lone Ranger.

30 "Never Say Die" (4/6/50). Clayton Moore, Jay Silverheels, Joseph Crehan, David Holt, Lee Phelps, Glenn Strange. Kidnapping the warden's son, Butch Cavendish breaks out of prison. Hot on his trail are the Lone Ranger and Tonto.

31 "Gold Fever" (4/13/50). Clayton Moore, Jay Silverheels, John Doucette, Francis Ford, George Lewis, Leonard Strong. Ox Martin robs a stagecoach. The Lone Ranger believes more than cash loot is involved.

32 "Death Trap" (4/20/50). Clayton Moore, Jay Silverheels, Kenne Duncan, James Griffith, Lucien Littlefield, Jeff York. Investigating the disappearance of three deputies, the Ranger's search takes him to the cabin of an old prospector.

33 "A Matter of Courage" (4/27/50). Clayton Moore, Jay Silverheels, James Arness, Edmund Cobb, Juan Duvall, Don Haggerty. Outlaws Farrel and Hinshaw attempt to flee across the border. A timid barber helps Tonto and the Ranger go after them.

34 "Rifles and Renegades" (5/4/50). Clayton Moore, Jay Silverheels, Robert Bice, John Hart, I. Stanford Jolley, Robert Kent, Gene Roth. An Army lieutenant is accused of selling rifles to the Indians. Tonto and the Lone Ranger must find the real culprit.

35 "Bullets for Ballots" (5/11/50). Clayton Moore, Jay Silverheels, John Alvin, Marjorie Lord, Craig Stevens, Frederic Tozere. A gang tries to interfere in a town's mayoral election. The Ranger and Tonto turn up to make sure things are done the right way.

36 "The Black Hat" (5/18/50). Clayton Moore, Jay Silverheels, John Eldredge, Ed Hinton, George Pembroke, Jeff York. After gold is stolen by bandits, the Lone Ranger has trouble picking up their trail. A black hat provides a clue.

37 "Devil's Pass" (5/25/50). Clayton Moore, Jay Silverheels, Jim Bannon, Marshall Bradford, Gene Evans, Jimmy Lloyd. A pair of red-headed men arouse Tonto and the Ranger's suspicions. A robbery does occur involving a red-headed man.

38 "Spanish Gold" (6/1/50). Clayton Moore, Jay Silverheels, Steve Clark, Gail Davis, Ross Ford, Kenneth Tobey. Framing a man for murder, outlaws try to find hidden gold by threatening his daughter.

39 "Damsels in Distress" (6/8/50). Clayton Moore, Jay Silverheels, John Banner, Phyllis Kennedy, Peggy McIntire, Tom Tyler, Gloria Winters. A criminal endangers three young women. To save them, the Ranger dons the disguise of an old Rebel soldier.

40 "Man Without a Gun" (6/15/50). Clayton Moore, Jay Silverheels, Eddie Dunn, James Harrison, Dick Jones, Ralph Moody. Homesteaders and Indians clash. Caught between the two sides are Tonto and the Lone Ranger.

41 "Pardon for Curley" (6/22/50). Clayton Moore, Jay Silverheels, Stephen Chase, Harry Harvey, Douglas Kennedy, Marion Martin. Breaking out of prison, Curley wants revenge. His targets are the Lone Ranger and Tonto.

42 "Eye for an Eye (6/26/50). Clayton Moore, Jay Silverheels, Steve Clark, John Day, Sue England, Chris-Pin Martin. The governor's daughter is threatened by outlaw Stark Durfee. Tonto and the Ranger intervene.

43 "Outlaws of the Plains" (7/6/50). Clayton Moore, Jay Silverheels, Edward Cassidy, Jack Lee, Bernie Marcus, Jay Morley. Sheriff Lem Shattuck is secretly involved with cattle rustling. It is up to the Lone Ranger to expose him.

44 "White Man's Magic" (7/13/50). Clayton Moore, Jay Silverheels, Lane Bradford, Jane Frazee, Bill Kennedy, Ralph Moody. An artist is framed for the murder of an Indian chief. Tonto and the Ranger must protect the artist from tribal revenge.

45 "Trouble for Tonto" (7/20/50). Clayton Moore, Jay Silverheels, Robert Arthur, Russ Conklin, Byron Foulger, Gene Roth, Lyle Talbot. The Lone Ranger wants to capture bad man Buck Fargo. In disguise as a chief to help route the man, Tonto's safety is threatened.

46 "Sheriff of Gunstock" (7/27/50). Clayton Moore, Jay Silverheels, John Doucette, John Hart, Walter Sande, William Vincent. The sheriff's son is kidnapped to keep Rocky Hanford's protection racket going.

47 "The Wrong Man" (8/3/50). Clayton Moore, Jay Silverheels, Don Beddoe, Richard Crane, Nan Leslie, Glen Vernon. Townsfolk think John Meredith committed murder. The Ranger and Tonto feel differently.

48 "The Beeler Gang" (8/10/50). Clayton Moore, Jay Silverheels, Beverly Garland, B.G. Norman, Ralph Peters, Robert Rockwell. Stan

Beeler's gang, trying to force a lawman to resign, kidnaps his son. The Lone Ranger dons a disguise to come to the rescue.

49 "The Star Witness" (9/17/50). Clayton Moore, Jay Silverheels, Ray Bennett, Michael Chapin, Gene Evans, Sarah Padden. Young Johnnie Williams saw a murder but no one will believe him. No one, that is, except for the Lone Ranger and Tonto.

50 "The Black Widow" (8/24/50). Clayton Moore, Jay Silverheels, John Alvin, Holly Bane, Lane Chandler, George Pembroke. A dead man's vest is a vital clue for the Lone Ranger. Both stolen money and a killer need to be found.

51 "The Whimsical Bandit" (8/31/50). Clayton Moore, Jay Silverheels, Chuck Courtney, Bud Osborne, Nestor Paiva, Sheila Ryan. The Ranger uses a bullwhip and a ring to stop outlaw Juan Branco.

Jay Silverheels' Tonto and Clayton Moore's Lone Ranger were two of the most recognized figures in the entertainment industry.

52 "Double Jeopardy" (9/7/50). Clayton Moore, Jay Silverheels, Jack Ingram, James Kirkwood, Christine Larson, Marin Sais. A judge's daughter is kidnapped to force the release of a man accused of murder.

Second Season (Episodes 53–78; Black and White)

53 "Million Dollar Wallpaper" (9/14/50). Clayton Moore, Jay Silverheels, Paul Fix, Lucien Littlefield, Emmett Lynn, Kim Spalding, Duke York. Wallpaper used in an old man's shack proves to be valuable stocks. When he is then threatened by crooks, the Lone Ranger comes to his aid.

54 "Mission Bells" (9/21/50). Clayton Moore, Jay Silverheels, Tristram Coffin, Hal Baylor, James Griffith, Lee Roberts, Walter Sande. A mystery lies behind a dishonest land speculator and two mission bells. Tonto and the Ranger are up to the challenge.

55 "Dead Man's Chest" (9/28/50). Clayton Moore, Jay Silverheels, Myron Healey, Harry Lauter, George Lloyd, William Vedder. An old prospector is killed by outlaws over a wooden chest. The outlaws must then deal with the Lone Ranger.

56 "Outlaw's Revenge" (10/5/50). Clayton Moore, Jay Silverheels, Larry J. Blake, William Haade, Larry Johns, Kenneth MacDonald. Banker Calvin Blair leads a double life as desperado Trigger Taylor. He plans on killing the Lone Ranger.

57 "Danger Ahead" (10/12/50). Clayton Moore, Jay Silverheels, Holly Bane, William E. Green, Don Haggerty, Max Terhune. A ventriloquist, Boswell, witnesses a sheriff's murder. The Ranger and Tonto help to bring the killer to justice.

58 "Crime in Time" (10/19/50). Clayton Moore, Jay Silverheels, Monte Blue, John A. Butler, Lane Bradford, Fred Libby. A counterfeiting jeweler gets involved with one of the infamous Watkins brothers. On their trail are Tonto and the Ranger.

59 "Drink of Water" (10/26/50). Clayton Moore, Jay Silverheels, Stanley Andrews, Harlan Briggs, Bill Kennedy, Mickey Simpson. The town of Greenville is suffering from a drought. Posing as rainmakers, bad men connive to kill the Lone Ranger and Tonto.

60 "Thieves' Money" (11/2/50). Clayton Moore, Jay Silverheels, Ward Blackburn, Jack Briggs, John Doucette, David McMahon. Counterfeiter Dumont is not above murder when anyone tries to get in his way. This includes Tonto and the Ranger.

61 "The Squire" (11/9/50). Clayton Moore, Jay Silverheels, John Cliff, Steve Dunhill, Margaret Kerry, Robert J. Wilke. The Lone Ranger and Tonto are after a gang of bank robbers. A town's leading citizen may be the mastermind behind the gang.

62 "Masked Deputy" (11/16/50). Clayton Moore, Jay Silverheels, Lane Chandler, Edmund Cobb, Stuart Randall, Carol Thurston, Dave Willock. Businessman Will Bradley is mixed up with cattle rustlers. The Lone Ranger and an old sheriff, Higgins, fight against them.

63 "Banker's Choice" (11/23/50). Clayton Moore, Jay Silverheels, David Bruce, John Merton, Phyllis Morris, Mickey Simpson. Banker McFarland is misled by blackmailers into believing his son is a thief. Tonto and the Ranger rally to the banker's side.

64 "Desert Adventure" (11/30/50). Clayton Moore, Jay Silverheels, Lane Bradford, Charles Horvath, House Peters, Jr., Lee Shumway. On the trail of the notorious Yuma Kid, Tonto and the Lone Ranger ride into scorching desert country.

65 "Bad Medicine" (12/7/50). Clayton Moore, Jay Silverheels, Hal Baylor, Dick Curtis, Greta Granstedt, Harry Harvey. The Bolton gang is holding a doctor hostage. To trick the gang, the Lone Ranger disguises himself as an Italian immigrant.

66 "One Jump Ahead" (12/14/50). Clayton Moore, Jay Silverheels, Richard Crane, John Eldredge, Robert Rockwell, Dorothy Vaughn. Outlaw Rick Sanders and his partner cheat the kin of Civil War victims. The Ranger and Tonto are out to stop them.

67 "Lady Killer" (12/21/50). Clayton Moore, Jay Silverheels, I. Stanford Jolley, Robert Kent, Nan Leslie, Fred Libby. Actress Lela Anson is behind murders and robberies. The Lone Ranger intends to stop her.

68 "Paid in Full" (12/28/50). Clayton Moore, Jay Silverheels, Larry J. Blake, John Day, Harry Lauter, Wanda McKay. The mortgage holder of Jim Craig's ranch tries to cheat him out of it. The Ranger and Tonto have other plans for the crook.

69 "Letter of the Law" (1/4/51). Clayton Moore, Jay Silverheels, Monte Blue, Warren Douglas, Ed Hinton, Noel Neill. Rancher Jeff Niles was once an outlaw. When he has trouble with an old cohort, he gets support from the Lone Ranger.

70 "The Silent Voice" (1/11/51). Clayton Moore, Jay Silverheels, Hal Baylor, Mira McKinney, Ross Ford, Mike Ragan. The Ranger is not about to let a trio of killers get away. Yet the only witness against them is an elderly woman who cannot speak or write.

71 "The Outcast" (1/18/51). Clayton Moore, Jay Silverheels, Lane Bradford, Edmund Cobb, Denver Pyle, Robert Rockwell, Mickey Simpson. Texas Rangers plan on capturing a gang of outlaws. But not without the Lone Ranger's help.

72 "Backtrail" (1/25/51). Clayton Moore, Jay Silverheels, Robert Bice, Riley Hill, Rex Lease, Kim Spalding. Tonto and the Lone Ranger try to protect Walter Mason's express business against theft. But Mason and his gang are really behind the wrongdoing.

73 "Behind the Law" (2/1/51). Clayton Moore, Jay Silverheels, Marshall Bradford, Robert Carson, George Chesebro, Gene Evans. Leading a double life, Jim Folsom is a lawful citizen in one place and runs an outlaw gang in another. Tonto and the Ranger prove to be his undoing.

74 "Trouble at Black Rock" (2/8/51). Clayton Moore, Jay Silverheels, John Alvin, Michael Ansara, George Lewis, Wanda McKay. An old-timer, Neely, finds gold coins hidden away. An escaped convict wants them back. Forced to intervene is the Lone Ranger.

75 "Two Gold Lockets" (2/15/51). Clayton Moore, Jay Silverheels, Stanley Andrews, Darryl Hickman, Dwayne Hickman, Ben Welden. A boy abducted and raised by outlaws is saved from becoming one. A pair of lockets help the Ranger and Tonto to reunite him with his father, a lawman.

76 "The Hooded Men" (2/22/50). Clayton Moore, Jay Silverheels, Lane Bradford, John Doucette, Mira McKinney, Denver Pyle,

Walter Sande. Outlaw gang members disguise themselves in their robberies. The Ranger dons the same disguise to entrap them.

77 "Friend in Need" (3/1/51). Clayton Moore, Jay Silverheels, Robert Bice, Edmund Cobb, Gail Davis, John McGuire. An innocent man is to be hanged. Going after the real guilty man, Luke Banner, is the Lone Ranger.

78 "Mr. Trouble" (3/8/51). Clayton Moore, Jay Silverheels, Jim Bannon, Larry J. Blake, Earle Hodgins, Robert Rockwell. Rick Merrill will lose his franchise with the railroad if he does not receive help. That help comes from the Lone Ranger and Tonto.

Third Season (Episodes 79–130; Black and White)

79 "Outlaw's Son" (9/11/52). John Hart, Jay Silverheels, Robert Arthur, John Pickard, Robert Rockwell, Irene Vernon. After his prison release, a former outlaw finds his own son trying to kill him. Tonto and the Ranger attempt to reunite the family.

80 "Outlaw Underground" (9/18/52). John Hart, Jay Silverheels, Michael Ansara, Robert Clarke, Lois Hall, Richard Reeves. A newspaperman gets tangled up with outlaws. The Lone Ranger must untangle the mess.

81 "Special Edition" (9/25/52). John Hart, Jay Silverheels, Larry Blake, Hal K. Dawson, Judd Holdren, Nan Leslie. Cave Creek's newspaper publisher plans to expose an outlaw gang. Protecting him from the gang are Tonto and the Masked Man.

82 "Desperado at Large" (10/2/52). John Hart, Jay Silverheels, James Brown, Steve Clark, Douglas Kennedy, Lee Van Cleef. A Federal agent, trying to catch a criminal, must also deal with a lynch mob. The Ranger and Tonto help him on both fronts.

83 "Through the Wall" (10/9/52). John Hart, Jay Silverheels, Douglas Evans, Dabbs Greer, George Lynn, Mike Ragan. Old Toby built a secret exit in a town's jail. To atone for it, he assists the Lone Ranger going after a criminal.

84 "Jeb's Gold Mine" (10/16/52). John Hart, Jay Silverheels, Lane Bradford, Robert Bray, Raymond Greenleaf, Syd Saylor. Gold is discovered on an old homesteader's land. The Lone Ranger helps him against opportunists out to cheat him.

85 "Frame for Two" (10/23/52). John Hart, Jay Silverheels, Richard Crane, John Damler, Robert Livingston, James Parnell. Taking advantage of a feud between two ranchers, a bad man kills one and lets the blame fall on the other. Tonto and the Ranger expose the frame-up and the killer.

86 "Ranger in Danger" (10/30/52). John Hart, Jay Silverheels, Robert Arthur, Douglas Kennedy. A boy is tricked into helping a killer who wants to trap the Lone Ranger and Tonto.

87 "Delayed Action" (I1–6–52). John Hart, Jay Silverheels, Stanley Andrews, James Griffith, Billy Vincent, Ben Weiden. A sheriff accuses Tonto and the Ranger of committing a robbery. Flint Taylor and his cronies are the real thieves.

88 "The Map" (11/13/52). John Hart, Jay Silverheels, Steve Darrell, Lanny Rees, Geraldine Wall, Frank Wilcox. To discover what land a railroad will use, crooks steal a map. A boy with an interest in chemistry helps the Ranger thwart them.

89 "Trial by Fire" (11/20/52). John Hart, Jay Silverheels, Stanley Andrews, Gail Davis, Mickey Simpson, Pierre Watkin, Robert J. Wilke. A man's son is accused of shooting him. The Ranger and Tonto go after the outlaw family responsible.

90 "The Pledge" (11/27/52). John Hart, Jay Silverheels, Harry Cheshire, Ross Elliott, Sam Flint, Hayden Rorke. A young rancher tricks a sheriff into releasing him after a frame-up by crooks. The Ranger must straighten matters out.

91 "Treason at Dry Creek" (12/4/52). John Hart, Jay Silverheels, Rand Brooks, Robert Carson, Ann Doran, Frank Fenton. Army dispatches are being sold to Indians at a Pony Express station. Tonto and the Ranger have to act fast to prevent disaster.

92 "The Condemned Man" (12/11/52). John Hart, Jay Silverheels, Don Beddoe, Monte Blue, Myron Healey, Russell Hicks. An Indian chief's son is murdered and an innocent man framed. Finding the guilty man is the Lone Ranger's job.

93 "The New Neighbor" (12/19/52). John Hart, Jay Silverheels, John Alvin, B.G. Norman, Walter Sande, Barbara Woodell. A new rancher becomes involved in a dispute with his neighbors over water rights. Attempting to resolve the problem are the Lone Ranger and Tonto.

94 "Best Laid Plans" (12/25/52). John Hart, Jay Silverheels, John Bryant, Cathy Downs, Judd Holdren, House Peters, Jr. Tension increases between neighbors in Sunset Valley when a gang tries to elect one of its own as sheriff. Tonto and the Ranger step in.

95 "Indian Charlie" (1/1/53). John Hart, Jay Silverheels, Sally Corner, Walter Reed, Glenn Strange, Alan Wells. An Indian boy turns against the white folks who raised him. The Ranger intervenes.

96 "The Empty Strongbox" (1/8/53). John Hart, Jay Silverheels, Robert Carson, Don Mahin, Hugh Prosser, James Todd. A trap with a bomb is set up by officials to stop stagecoach robbers. The Ranger and Tonto are also endangered by it.

97 "Trader Boggs" (1/15/53). John Hart, Jay Silverheels, Kenne Duncan, I. Stanford Jolley, Hal Price, Aline Towne. The Lone Ranger's old friend Barnaby Boggs is in trouble: Attempting to open a store, he faces an unscrupulous rival.

98 "Bandits in Uniform" (1/22/53). John Hart, Jay Silverheels, Robert Bray, John Doucette, I. Stanford Jolley, James Parnell. An American dictator and his henchmen over-tax Mexican settlers. Tonto and the Ranger support the oppressed.

99 "The Godless Men" (1/29/53). John Hart, Jay Silverheels, Hugh Beaumont, Ray Page, Keith Richards, Hugh Sanders. The lawless element in Gold City steal from the church. Preacher Roberts turns to the Lone Ranger for assistance.

100 "The Devil's Bog" (2/5/53). John Hart, Jay Silverheels, Van Des Autels, Harry Harvey, Hugh Prosser, Barbara Woodell. A swamp's mosquitoes make Tonto ill. The Ranger helps a doctor drain the swamp.

101 "Right to Vote" (2/12/53). John Hart, Jay Silverheels, John Damler, Dick Elliott, Douglas Kennedy, Ben Welden. The Lone Ranger and Tonto must find stolen petitions to remove crooks from political office.

102 "The Sheriff's Son" (2/19/53). John Hart, Jay Silverheels, Claudia Barrett, William Haade, Hugh Prosser, Alan Wells. A sheriff faces the wrath of an outlaw, his own son. The Ranger counsels the troubled young man.

103 "Tumblerock Law" (2/26/53). John Hart, Jay Silverheels, Steve Brodie, Richard Crane, Byron Foulger, Tom London. A witness to the sheriff's murder is kidnapped by town bos, Ace Broderick. Only the Ranger and Tonto can restore order.

104 "Sinner by Proxy" (3/5/53). John Hart, Jay Silverheels, Stephen Chase, Russ Conway, Ross Elliott, Hugh Sanders, Mickey Simpson. An outlaw poses as the Ranger to rob the Johnsville bank. The real Ranger must prove his innocence, and that of a man who gave false information.

105 "A Stage for Mademoiselle" (3/12/53). John Hart, Jay Silverheels, Lane Bradford, Edmund Cobb, Noreen Nash, Frank Wilcox. An opera singer plans to have her jewels stolen as a publicity stunt. When they are actually taken, Tonto and the Ranger offer their assistance.

106 "A Son by Adoption" (3/19/53). John Hart, Jay Silverheels, William Challee, Russ Conway, Peter Mamakos, Frank Richards. Trying to keep the truth from an adopted boy is no easy matter for the Lone Ranger: The boy's real father is an outlaw.

107 "Mrs. Banker" (3/26/53). John Hart, Jay Silverheels, Steve Mitchell, Robert Neil [Scott Elliott], Esther Somers, Dan White. The Ranger and Tonto investigate a rash of stage robberies. The masked man's old prospector disguise is put to good use.

108 "Trouble in Town" (4/2/53). John Hart, Jay Silverheels, Ross Ford, Dayton Lummis, Mira McKinney, Lyle Talbot. A banker, Wilkins, is worried that his institution will fold following a robbery.

109 "Black Gold" (4/9/53). John Hart, Jay Silverheels, Jim Hayward, Todd Karns, Robert Shayne, William Vedder. Outlaws beat up a geologist and plan on stealing another man's oil rights. The Lone Ranger has other ideas.

110 "The Durango Kid" (4/16/53). John Hart, Jay Silverheels, James Griffith, Judd Holdren, Nan Leslie, Lee Shumway. A woman from the East mistakes an outlaw for a long-lost brother. The Ranger and Tonto find her real sibling.

111 "The Deserter" (4/23/53). John Hart, Jay Silverheels, Lane Bradford, Rand Brooks, Chuck Courtney, Robert Foulk, Keith Richards. A soldier regrets deserting the Army. To redeem himself, he aids Tonto, the Ranger and the latter's nephew, Dan Reid, battle outlaws.

112 "Embezzler's Harvest" (4/30/53). John Hart, Jay Silverheels, Stephen Chase, Leonard Freeman, Lois Hall, Harry Harvey. Two baddies get involved with embezzling funds for an irrigation project—and murder.

113 "El Toro" (5/7/53). John Hart, Jay Silverheels, Richard Avonde, Chuck Courtney, Jim Hayward, Gene Wesson. A bandit, El Toro, is saved by Dan Reid. When Dan, the Ranger and Tonto need help, the favor is returned.

114 "The Brown Pony" (5/14/53). John Hart, Jay Silverheels, Adele Longmire, Dennis Ross, Charles Stevens, Lee Van Cleef. A father is charged with a crime and his family tries to exonerate him. The mother is even ready to sell their son's pony to do so.

115 "Triple Cross" (5/21/53). John Hart, Jay Silverheels, John Cliff, Fred Coby, Jack Ingram, Judy Nugent. An escaped convict is murdered for his stolen loot. The one witness, a young lady, must be protected by the Lone Ranger.

116 "Wake of War" (5/28/53). John Hart, Jay Silverheels, Don Beddoe, Richard Crane, Hugh Prosser, Sheb Wooley. Wanting to keep Civil War veterans fighting with each other, gamblers frame a man for murder.

117 "Death in the Forest" (6/4/53). John Hart, Jay Silverheels, John Damler, Raymond Greenleaf, Judd Holdren, DeForest Kelley, Mickey Simpson. Tonto and the Ranger discover a plot to kill a state governor. The governor's aide is involved.

118 "Gentlemen from Julesburg" (6/11/53). John Hart, Jay Silverheels, Nan Leslie, Robert Neil [Scott Elliott], Walter Reed, Eddy

Waller. Crooks frame a young man for a robbery. The Lone Ranger enlists the help of a down-on-his-luck gambler.

119 "Hidden Fortune" (6/18/53). John Hart, Jay Silverheels, Steve Darrell, Ann Doran, I. Stanford Jolley, Bruce Payne. After ten years in prison for robbery, two men find a house has been built over their hidden loot.

120 "The Old Cowboy" (6/25/53), John Hart, Jay Silverheels, Steve Brodie, Frank Fenton, Denver Pyle, Russell Simpson. His eyesight failing, an old-timer is a perfect target for crooks wanting to cheat him.

121 "Woman from Omaha" (7/2/53). John Hart, Jay Silverheels, Harry Harvey, Charles Horvath, Minerva Urecal, Terry Wilson. Taking over her late brother's stagecoach line is not easy for Nell Martin, but Tonto and the Ranger are there to help.

122 "Gunpowder Joe" (7/9/53). John Hart, Jay Silverheels, Stanley Blystone, Chubby Johnson, Frank Richards, Glenn Strange. The Lone Ranger and his Indian companion aid Gunpowder Joe, an old explosives expert. It seems Butch Cavendish is back stirring up trouble.

123 "The Midnight Rider" (7/16/53). John Hart, Jay Silverheels, Harry Cheshire, Steve Darrell, Darryl Hickman, Mickey Simpson, Harry Woods. A young man is forced to become an outlaw called the Midnight Rider.

124 "Stage to Estacado" (7/23/53). John Hart, Jay Silverheels, Phyllis Coates, Ian MacDonald, Lee Van Cleef, Sheb Wooley. Tonto and the Masked Man help a young couple with a new stage line. Their competition proves to be dishonest and ruthless.

125 "The Perfect Crime" (7/30/53). John Hart, Jay Silverheels, Robert Bray, Phyllis Coates, Edna Holland, Hayden Rorke. A schoolteacher's life is in jeopardy when she learns of a bank robbery scheme.

126 "The Ghost of Coyote Canyon" (8/6/53). John Hart, Jay Silverheels, Richard Alexander, Lucien Littlefield, Tom London, Marshall Reed, Hank Worden. To keep townsfolk away from their hideout, thieves pretend it is haunted. That does not stop the Ranger or Tonto.

127 "Old Bailey" (8/13/53). John Hart, Jay Silverheels, Bruce Cowling, Ray Montgomery, Steve Pendleton, Phil Tead. Gamblers frame a derelict, Old Bailey, for murdering a rancher. The Lone Ranger exposes the guilty parties.

128 "Prisoner in Jeopardy" (8/20/53). John Hart, Jay Silverheels, Stanley Blystone, Richard Crane, Dorothy Patrick, Frank Wilcox. After serving time for a crime he did not commit, a young man faces another frame-up.

129 "Diamond in the Rough" (8/27/53). John Hart, Jay Silverheels, Leo Britt, Harry Lauter, Emory Parnell, House Peters, Jr. A thief hides a diamond inside a ventriloquist's dummy. The Lone Ranger attempts to catch him and recover the jewel.

130 "The Red Mark" (9/3/53). John Hart, Jay Silverheels, Paul Bryar, Frank Fenton, Tom London, Alan Wells. The Ranger uses an Indian disguise to go after stagecoach robbers. The stolen bills have red marks on them.

Fourth Season (Episodes 131–182; Black and White)

131 "The Fugitive" (9/9/54). Clayton Moore, Jay Silverheels, Griff Barnett, John Doucette, Paul Langton, Denver Pyle. With a mob threatening him, Clay Trowbridge—falsely charged with murder—escapes from jail. The Ranger and Tonto are sent after him.

132 "Ex-Marshal" (9/15/54). Clayton Moore, Jay Silverheels, Stanley Clements, Tyler McVey, Glenn Strange, Ray Teal. Former lawman Frank Dean believes he's lost his nerves. The Ranger proves otherwise.

133 "Message to Fort Apache" (9/23/54). Clayton Moore, Jay Silverheels, Lane Bradford, Chick Chandler, Nancy Hale, Robert Livingston, Sheb Wooley. Outlaws sell guns to hostile Indians. The Ranger and Tonto help the Army put a stop to it.

134 "The Frightened Woman" (9/30/54). Clayton Moore, Jay Silverheels, Emlen Davies, Emmett Lynn, Ricky Murray, Richard Travis. A widow's life is in danger after she witnesses a robbery. Riding to her aid is the Lone Ranger.

135 "Gold Town" (10/7/54). Clayton Moore, Jay Silverheels, Edward Ashley, Myron Healey, Earle Hodgins, Pierre Watkin. A prospector dies, leaving his money to the Ranger and Englishman Edgar Wellington. An outlaw schemes to get part of the inheritance.

136 "Six Gun Sanctuary" (10/14/54). Clayton Moore, Jay Silverheels, Hal Baylor, Don Beddoe, Frank Fenton, Douglas Kennedy. The town of Reidsville is used as a sanctuary by outlaws. The Lone Ranger and Tonto help a sheriff restore law and order.

137 "Outlaw's Trail" (10/21/54). Clayton Moore, Jay Silverheels, Robert Bice, Robert Bray, Christian Drake, Jack Elam. Gunmen Reno Lawrence and Joe Tarbuck are stirring up trouble, but Tonto and the Ranger are more than a match for them.

138 "Stage to Teshimingo" (10/28/54). Clayton Moore, Jay Silverheels, Lane Bradford, Mira McKinney, Don Megowan, Ben Welden, Hank Worden. A stage line is threatened with ruin by a series of robberies. Called in to help stop them are the Masked Man and Tonto.

139 "Texas Draw" (11/4/54). Clayton Moore, Jay Silverheels, Christopher Dark, Barry Kelley, Marion Ross, James Westerfield. Gunman Crane Dillon covets rich copper deposits on land owned by a reverend. Standing in the gunman's way: the Lone Ranger.

140 "Rendezvous at Whipsaw" (11/11/54). Clayton Moore, Jay Silverheels, Don Beddoe, John Doucette, William Haade, Hugh Sanders. After a brother and sister get into trouble, the Ranger and Tonto are there for them.

141 "Dan Reid's Fight for Life" (11/18/54). Clayton Moore, Jay Silverheels, Chuck Courtney, Henry Kulky, Nestor Paiva, Mickey Simpson. Tonto and the Lone Ranger are after the Cardoza gang. The gang takes Dan Reid captive.

142 "Tenderfoot" (11/25/54). Clayton Moore, Jay Silverheels, Hal Baylor, William Forrest, Robert Horton, Dan Riss. Jim Ferris runs into trouble over the sale of his ranch.

143 "A Broken Match" (12/2/54). Clayton Moore, Jay Silverheels, Whit Bissell, Fred Coby, Glen Gordon, Nan Leslie. Ex-con Jeff Williams is falsely accused of criminal activities. Match sticks are clues which lead the Lone Ranger to the real culprits.

144 "Colorado Gold" (12/9/54). Clayton Moore, Jay Silverheels, Claudia Barrett, Gil Donaldson, Gene Roth, Robert Shayne. The Maybelle Mine is producing ore and Luther Gage's greed gets the best of him.

145 "Homer with a High Hat" (12/16/54). Clayton Moore, Jay Silverheels, Tom Brown, Chick Chandler, Kathleen Crowley, Minerva Urecal. An Easterner has trouble with his niece's fiancé (a marshal) and an outlaw gang.

146 "Two for Juan Ringo" (12/23/54). Clayton Moore, Jay Silverheels, Robert Bray, Bob Cason, John Hoyt, Lyle Talbot. A shady Englishman runs Border City. Disguised as outlaw Juan Ringo, the Ranger investigates.

147 "The Globe" (12/30/54). Clayton Moore, Jay Silverheels, Frank Ferguson, Gregg Palmer, Stuart Randall, Michael Whalen. An injured bank clerk, Stan Ammons, is found by Tonto and the Ranger. The three expose bank fraud in the town of Oreville.

148 "Dan Reid's Sacrifice" (1/6/55). Clayton Moore, Jay Silverheels, Chuck Courtney, Fred Graham, Percy Helton, Bill Kennedy. Dan Reid attempts to help the Lone Ranger and Tonto capture horse thieves. His own horse, Victor, is stolen.

149 "Enfield Rifle" (1/13/55). Clayton Moore, Jay Silverheels, Rand Brooks, Walter Coy, Frank Ferguson, Maurice Jara. When new repeating rifles fall into the hands of renegade Indians, there's fear of an uprising. The Ranger and Tonto help the Army prevent it.

150 "The School Story" (1/20/55). Clayton Moore, Jay Silverheels, Lee Aaker, Stanley Andrews, John Doucette, Dick Elliott, Madge Meredith. The Ranger has to convince a boy, Tommy Righter, how important an education will be.

151 "The Quiet Highwayman" (1/27/55). Clayton Moore, Jay Silverheels, Chuck Courtney, Harry Harvey, Francis McDonald, Hugh Sanders. A hooded desperado is creating unrest amongst the townsfolk of Bakersville, and a marshal needs the Ranger's help.

152 "The Heritage of Treason" (2/3/55). Clayton Moore, Jay Silverheels, Don Haggerty, Ed Hinton, Stuart Randall, Peter Whitney. Ruling over Arizona is the goal of cattle king Halstead and his gang.

153 "The Lost Chalice" (2/10/55). Clayton Moore, Jay Silverheels, William Challee, James Griffith, Julian Rivero, Joseph Turkel. Mission Valley's padre needs help finding a water supply and keeping a gold chalice out of the hands of escaped convicts.

154 "Code of the Pioneers" (2/17/55). Clayton Moore, Jay Silverheels, Chuck Courtney, Emlen Davies, Harry Lauter, Lyle Talbot. A Gold Creek newspaperwoman and the Ranger contend with a politico who wants to steal an election.

155 "The Law Lady" (2/24/55). Clayton Moore, Jay Silverheels, Don Garrett, Peter Hansen, Marjorie Lord, Richard Travis. A young lady steps forward to do her sheriff-husband's job after he is killed.

156 "Uncle Ed" (3/3/55). Clayton Moore, Jay Silverheels, Will Wright, Peter Mamakos, June Whitley, Nadine Ashdown. An old farmer loves to make up stories. One, however, involves him and the Lone Ranger and it's true.

157 "Jornado del Muerto" (3/10/55). Clayton Moore, Jay Silverheels, Richard Crane, John Hubbard, Rick Vallin, Joseph Vitale. The outlaw, Cantrell, is living with Apache Indians. It is up to the Ranger and Tonto to find him.

158 "Sunstroke Mesa" (3/17/55). Clayton Moore, Jay Silverheels, Chuck Courtney, Joseph Crehan, Dwayne Hickman, John Pickard. The Ranger brings outlaws to justice and helps a wayward teenager.

159 "Sawtelle Saga's End" (3/24/55). Clayton Moore, Jay Silverheels, Frances Bavier, Robert Fouik, Peter Hansen, Paul Keast. Trailing bank robbers, Tonto and the Ranger arrive at the farm of an elderly woman, Aunt Maggie. She turns out to be the leader of the thieves.

160 "The Too-Perfect Signature" (3/31/55). Clayton Moore, Jay Silverheels, Stacy Keach, Charles Meredith, Glenn Strange, Ray Teal. A crooked lawyer forges a rancher's name to a deed. The Ranger is there to aid the rancher.

161 "Trigger Finger" (4/7/55). Clayton Moore, Jay Silverheels, Chuck Courtney, Laura Elliott, Stacy Keach, Douglas Kennedy, Mickey Simpson. Dan Reid and the Ranger help Sheriff Trent, who has been accused of shooting an innocent man.

162 "The Tell-Tale Bullet" (4/14/55). Clayton Moore, Jay Silverheels, Anthony Caruso, John Cason, Roy Roberts, Dennis Weaver. A country doctor's son is implicated in a bank robbery.

163 "False Accusations" (4/21/55). Clayton Moore, Jay Silverheels, Whit Bissell, Robert Bray, Harry Harvey, Michael Whalen. In Rock Point, the Ranger is mistaken for a bank robber. Tonto comes to the aid of his friend.

164 "Gold Freight" (4/28/55). Clayton Moore, Jay Silverheels, Chuck Courtney, Ted DeCorsia, Kenneth MacDonald, House Peters, Jr. The Ranger, Tonto and Dan Reid rally to the aid of a freight line operator. A dishonest competitor is making things hard for him.

165 "Wanted: The Lone Ranger" (5/5/55). Clayton Moore, Jay Silverheels, Richard Travis, Jesse White, Sheb Wooley, James Courtney. The Ranger pretends to be a clown in a show in order to catch the gang framing him for their criminal activities.

166 "The Woman in the White Mask" (5/12/55). Clayton Moore, Jay Silverheels, Phyllis Coates, Chuck Courtney, Denver Pyle, Richard Reeves. Holding a miner responsible for their father's death, a sister and brother seek vengeance. The Ranger and Dan Reid show them the error of their ways.

167 "Bounty Hunter" (5/19/55). Clayton Moore, Jay Silverheels, Russ Conway, Gil Fallman, Richard Reeves, Pierre Watkin. The Bolton gang and a bounty hunter, Lex Sharp, scheme to get their hands on reward money. Tonto and the Masked Man run interference.

168 "Showdown at Sand Creek" (5/26/55). Clayton Moore, Jay Silverheels, Paul Burke, Stacy Keach, Phil Tead, Robert B. Williams. The Lone Ranger learns that the Sand Creek sheriff has been killed. The lawman's brother needs help taking over the job.

169 "Heart of a Cheater" (6/9/55). Clayton Moore, Jay Silverheels, Chuck Courtney, Tommy Ivo, Natalie Masters, Eddy Waller.

Eyewitness to a bank robbery, Dan Reid joins up with the Lone Ranger to track the robbers.

170 "The Swami" (6/16/55). Clayton Moore, Jay Silverheels, Chuck Courtney, Kem Dibbs, Earle Hodgins, Lou Krugman, Eddy Waller. When Barnaby Boggs is cheated by a traveling swami, the Ranger and Dan Reid again join forces.

171 "Sheriff's Sale" (6/23/55). Clayton Moore, Jay Silverheels, Larry Blake, Thurston Hall, Peter Hansen, Helen Seamon. Sheriff Jack Morrison has his hands full dealing with outlaw Hutch Conant. Tonto and the Ranger are soon at the sheriff's side.

172 "Six-Gun Artist" (6/30/55). Clayton Moore, Jay Silverheels, Mort Mills, Elaine Riley, Guy Williams, Norman Willis. A young lady shows up in Mesa Junction where stage robberies are taking place.

173 "Death Goes to Press" (7/7/55). Clayton Moore, Jay Silverheels, Frank Ferguson, Peter Hansen, Kenneth MacDonald, Addison Richards. The local Cactus Creek newspaper gives the sheriff a hard time.

174 "Return of Dice Dawson" (7/14/55). Clayton Moore, Jay Silverheels, Harry Carey, Jr., Harry Lauter, Barbara Eiler, Herbert Heyes. Former outlaw Dice Dawson has changed his name and become a respected citizen. When he is accused of criminal activity, the Ranger steps in.

175 "Adventure at Arbuckle" (7/21/55). Clayton Moore, Jay Silverheels, William Challee, James Griffith, Nan Leslie, Ray Teal. An outlaw gang is behind the death of a newspaperman. Now the gang must contend with his daughter Susan Starr and the Lone Ranger.

176 "The Return" (7/28/55). Clayton Moore, Jay Silverheels, Christopher Dark, Yvette Dugay, Terry Frost, Frank Wilcox. Educated at a mission, a young Indian woman, Talana, returns home to learn that her brother is a renegade.

177 "Framed for Murder" (8/4/55). Clayton Moore, Jay Silverheels, James Best, Whit Bissell, David Bruce, Jan Shepard. Jim Blake makes a gold strike and becomes involved with a man bent on murder.

178 "Trapped" (8/11/55). Clayton Moore, Jay Silverheels, John Doucette, Taggart Casey, Robert Ellis, Frank Ferguson. Hardened Gaff Morgan and a younger man escape from prison. The Lone Ranger is soon on their trail.

179 "The Bait: Gold" (8/18/55). Clayton Moore, Jay Silverheels, Richard Avonde, Joan Hovis, George Neise, Michael Whalen, Hank Worden. The Ranger and Tonto go to the aid of a father and daughter whose gold shipments are targeted by outlaws.

180 "The Sheriff's Wife" (8/25/55). Clayton Moore, Jay Silverheels, John Bryant, Elaine Edwards, Jack Elam, Joseph Turkel. Going after a sheriff's two killers is a dangerous job for his wife. Also threatened by the killers are the Lone Ranger and his Indian companion.

181 "Counterfeit Redskins" (9/1/55). Clayton Moore, Jay Silverheels, John Doucette, Russell Johnson, Paul Langton, Harry Lauter. Three men disguised as Indians attempt to force homesteaders off their land. Tonto and the Ranger refuse to let this continue.

182 "One Nation, Indivisible" (9/8/55). Clayton Moore, Jay Silverheels, Roy Barcroft, Rand Brooks, Tyler MacDuff, Lyle Talbot. After they lose their farm in the Civil War, two brothers now face a crooked banker. The Lone Ranger restores their faith in the United States.

Fifth Season (Episodes 183–221; Color)

183 "The Wooden Rifle" (9/13/56). Clayton Moore, Jay Silverheels, Rand Brooks, Paul Engle, Barbara Knudson, Sydney Mason. Farmer Max Sunday is killed for his land by a man who then frames another for the crime. The Ranger goes undercover as a traveling salesman to investigate.

184 "The Sheriff of Smoke Tree" (9/20/56). Clayton Moore, Jay Silverheels, John Beradino, Ron Hagerthy, Tudor Owen, Slim Pickens, Mickey Simpson. Buck Webb, Smoke Tree's new sheriff, runs up against the Crater gang.

185 "The Counterfeit Mask" (9/27/56). Clayton Moore, Jay Silverheels, William Challee, John Cliff, Paul Engle, Sydney Mason. In Silver Springs, the Lone Ranger is accused of committing a number of crimes. He dons a disguise to capture the real perpetrator.

186 "No Handicap" (10/4/56). Clayton Moore, Jay Silverheels, John Beradino, Ron Hagerthy, Tudor Owen, Will Wright. Lawman Griff Allison is blinded by bank robbers. The Ranger's help includes giving the man hope.

187 "The Cross of Santo Domingo" (10/11/56). Clayton Moore, Jay Silverheels, Jeanne Bates, Lane Bradford, Johnny Crawford, Denver Pyle. An exquisite cross proves to be a temptation for both a jeweler and outlaws. Standing in their way are Tonto and the Masked Man.

188 "White Hawk's Decision" (10/18/56). Clayton Moore, Jay Silverheels, Edmund Hashim, Harry Lauter, Charles Stevens, Robert Swan. The hateful son of an Indian chief is killed by the outlaws he entrusted. The Lone Ranger must prevent warfare from breaking out over it.

189 "The Return of Don Pedro O'Sullivan" (10/25/56). Clayton Moore, Jay Silverheels, John Beradino, George J. Lewis, Tudor Owen, Mickey Simpson. A patriot risks his life to rid Mexico of its tyrants. Risking their lives to help are Tonto and the Ranger.

190 "Quicksand" (11/1/56). Clayton Moore, Jay Silverheels, Robert Burton, Terry Frost, Denver Pyle, Henry Rowland. A vile lawyer and an Indian renegade kill and steal in their lust for gold.

191 "Quarterhorse War" (11/8/56). Clayton Moore, Jay Silverheels, Harry Lauter, George Mather, Mae Morgan, William Tannen. A sheriff steals prize money from a race and frames another man for it. Conflict over the money involves Indians and must be resolved by the Lone Ranger.

192 "The Letter Bride" (11/15/56). Clayton Moore, Jay Silverheels, John Beradino, Judy Dan, Victor Sen Yung, Mickey Simpson. Some folks don't want Chinaman Lee Po and his mail order bride in the town of Forgens Flat.

193 "Hot Spell in Panamint" (11/22/56). Clayton Moore, Jay Silverheels, Rand Brooks, William Challee, Barbara Knudson, Sydney Mason. An outlaw gang makes things tough for lawman Roy Bell when he refuses to let a prisoner go.

194 "The Twisted Track" (11/29/56). Clayton Moore, Jay Silverheels, Gregg Barton, Robert Burton, Terry Frost, William Henry. Two brothers, ex-Confederate soldiers, seek to take revenge on a railroad owner.

195 "Decision for Chris McKeever" (12/6/56). Clayton Moore, Jay Silverheels, George Mather, Sandy Sanders, Robert Swan, William

Clayton Moore and Jay Silverheels took time out to endorse the Christmas Seals campaign in 1955.

Tannen. The McKeever gang robs a stagecoach and take Tonto and the Ranger prisoner. The youngest gang member, Chris McKeever, must decide where his loyalties lie.

196 "Trouble at Tylerville" (12/13/56). Clayton Moore, Jay Silverheels, Tom Brown, Mary Ellen Kay, Francis McDonald, John Pickard. The townsfolk in Tylerville don't want ex-convict Roy Hillman to live there. The Lone Ranger helps smooth things over.

197 "Christmas Story" (12/20/56). Clayton Moore, Jay Silverheels, Jimmy Baird, Lane Bradford, Robert Burton, Mary Newton, Aline Towne. Saddle maker Ben Talbot leaves his family for a get-rich-quick scheme. The Ranger and Tonto help bring everyone back together.

198 "Ghost Canyon" (12/27/56). Clayton Moore, Jay Silverheels, Edmund Hashim, Harry Lauter, Charles Stevens, Robert Swan. Bad men are after silver and create conflict between two Indian brothers.

199 "Outlaw Masquerade" (1/3/57). Clayton Moore, Jay Silverheels, Richard Crane, Joseph Crehan, House Peters, Jr., Steven Ritch. Disguised as an outlaw, the Ranger helps three robbers break out of jail. His motive: to find a stolen gold shipment.

200 "The Avenger" (1/10/57). Clayton Moore, Jay Silverheels, Roy Barcroft, Tristram Coffin, Francis McDonald, Alan Wells. After his father is killed, a son takes over the crusade to rid the town of outlaws.

201 "The Courage of Tonto" (1/17/57). Clayton Moore, Jay Silverheels, Joel Ashley, Jim Bannon, Maurice Jara, Francis McDonald. Tonto and the Ranger are involved in a dispute between Lew Pearson and Chief Gray Horse. When the chief is killed, his son blames the Masked Man.

202 "The Breaking Point" (1/24/57). Clayton Moore, Jay Silverheels, Richard Crane, Brad Morrow, Keith Richards, Charles Wagenheim. Outlaws hold a man captive for his gold claim. The man's young son turns to the Lone Ranger.

203 "A Harp for Hannah" (1/31/57). Clayton Moore, Jay Silverheels, Trevor Bardette, Louise Lewis, Pierce Lyden, Bob Roark. A farmer saves money to buy his wife a harp but it's stolen by a rancher's spoiled son.

204 "A Message from Abe" (2/7/57). Clayton Moore, Jay Silverheels, James Griffith, Mauritz Hugo, Maggie O'Byrne, Harry Strang. Ex-convict Phil Beach becomes desperate when his wife needs medical aid and her father will not help financially. The Lone Ranger intervenes.

205 "Code of Honor" (2/14/57). Clayton Moore, Jay Silverheels, Paul Engle, Rand Brooks, William Challee, John Cliff, Helene Marshall. An Army captain tangles with outlaws who want to get their hands on gold.

206 "The Turning Point" (2/21/57). Clayton Moore, Jay Silverheels, George Barrows, Paul Campbell, Pierce Lyden, Margaret Stewart. Crime is a problem in Blue River and vigilantes make the situation worse.

207 "Dead Eye" (2/28/57). Clayton Moore, Jay Silverheels, William Fawcett, Myron Healey, Nolan Leary, Zon Murray. Retired lawman Dallas "Dead Eye" Jones is on the comeback trail. At his side when he takes on a pair of outlaws are the Ranger and Tonto.

208 "Clover in the Dust" (3/7/57). Clayton Moore, Jay Silverheels, Dan Barton, Don C. Harvey, Sydney Mason, Harry Strang. A rancher's son is killed going after rustlers. But he left a clue for the Lone Ranger.

209 "Slim's Boy" (3/14/57). Clayton Moore, Jay Silverheels, Trevor Bardette, Louise Lewis, Pierce Lyden, Bob Roark. An old lawman deals with various problems which include arthritis and a past nemesis. The Ranger goes undercover to help.

210 "Two Against Two" (3/21/57). Clayton Moore, Jay Silverheels, Baynes Barron, Gary Murray, Eugenia Paul. Bank robber Vic Foley is also not above shooting his own partner in the back for their loot.

211 "Ghost Town Fury" (3/28/57). Clayton Moore, Jay Silverheels, Baynes Barron, Richard Crane, House Peters, Jr., Steven Ritch. Tonto and the Ranger must deal with the stagecoach-robbing Clanton brothers.

212 "The Prince of Buffalo Gap" (4/4/57). Clayton Moore, Jay Silverheels, Jim Bannon, Robert Crosson, Gabor Curtiz, Michael Winkleman. Visiting Buffalo Gap, young Prince Maximilian overhears his uncle plotting his death. The prince runs off and finds allies in the Masked Man and Tonto.

213 "The Law and Miss Aggie" (4/11/57). Clayton Moore, Jay Silverheels, Brad Jackson, Florence Lake, Dennis Moore, Joe Vitale. Indians killed Aggie Turner's husband and took their son. Now the Lone Ranger must convince her that the boy has been raised by them.

214 "The Tarnished Star" (4/18/57). Clayton Moore, Jay Silverheels, Paul Engle, William Fawcett, Myron Healey, Mercedes Shirley, Zon Murray. Peaceful Valley's lawman seems to be involved with masked robbers. Uncovering the truth is a task for the Ranger.

215 "Canuck" (4/25/57). Clayton Moore, Jay Silverheels, Roy Barcroft, Richard Benedict, Virginia Christine, Tristram Coffin. French-Canadian settlers are being cheated and killed by outlaws. The Lone Ranger disguises himself as a settler to stop it.

216 "Mission for Tonto" (5/2/57). Clayton Moore, Jay Silverheels, Lane Bradford, Robert Burton, Florence Lake, Tyler MacDuff. Two ex-cons and their mother target a rancher and his grandson.

217 "Journey to San Carlos" (5/9/57). Clayton Moore, Jay Silverheels, Melinda Byron, Myron Healey, Joe Sargent, Rick Vallin. Renegade Indians are on the warpath. Tonto and the Lone Ranger try to stop them. In doing so, they help two men to redeem themselves.

218 "The Banker's Son" (5/16/57). Clayton Moore, Jay Silverheels, Jim Bannon, Pat Lawless, Ewing Mitchell, Hank Worden. In Two Rivers, Tonto sees a banker shot by his own son—and then Tonto is blamed for the crime.

219 "The Angel and the Outlaw" (5/23/57). Clayton Moore, Jay Silverheels, Brad Jackson, Florence Lake, Dennis Moore, Linda Wrather. An older lady attempts to keep one of her orphaned charges from the outlaw trail.

220 "Blind Witness" (5/30/57). Clayton Moore, Jay Silverheels, William Fawcett, Byron Foulger, Myron Healey, Nolan Leary, Kay Riehl. Thieves caught red-handed by Tonto and the Ranger accuse *them* of the crime. One witness appears to be a blind old man.

221 "Outlaws in Greasepaint" (6/6/57). Clayton Moore, Jay Silverheels, Tom Brown, Mary Ellen Kay, John Pickard, Ben Welden. Wells Fargo gold shipments are being stolen. The Lone Ranger dons the disguise of a Shakespearean player to infiltrate an acting troupe of thieves.

ABC's *Lone Ranger* series certainly had an unusual format in that its original run on Thursday nights was spread over eight years. The five years of actual productions were interspersed with three of reruns, all between September 1949 and September 1957. However, while the series was still in production, ABC also aired reruns Friday nights (10–10:30) from June 1950 to September 1950. CBS also began showing reruns during the actual show's run, beginning in June 1953 on Saturday afternoons (1–1:30) and continuing until September 1958. The latter reruns were the shows I first remember seeing as a boy.

After production of the series ended, reruns on ABC continued between September 1957 and September 1960 on Sunday evenings (5:30–6). From September 1960 to September 1961, ABC reruns were aired (5:30–6 p.m.) on Wednesdays; and finally between March and September 1965, Saturday mornings from 10:30 to 11. Reruns on CBS also continued after the show ended: October 1958 to September 1959, Saturdays at 5–5:30 p.m.; and October 1959 to September 1960 on Saturday mornings. Between September 1966 and September 1969, CBS reruns were seen on Saturdays in different time slots. NBC was also in on the action. I remember its Saturday morning reruns between October 1960 and September 1961.

Between Republic's 1939 Lone Ranger serial and the TV series, George W. Trendle had not developed any further film adventures for the character. In the 1940s, Universal had shown interest. Trendle allowed for Universal to instead produce a pair of Green Hornet adventures.

Trendle, apparently cautious due to the way he felt Republic mistreated the character, bided his time and then turned to the new medium of television. With his company, Lone Ranger Inc., Trendle formed a partnership with producer Jack Chertok and his Apex Film Corporation; and like with the radio show (still being aired at the time), used its sponsor, General Mills, as the national sponsor for the ABC show. (Merita Bread was the sponsor in the southeastern United States.)

The Lone Ranger premiered on ABC on September 15, 1949. Just as the main character did for fledgling radio station WXYZ back in the 1930s, so too was ABC rescued. In 1950, this pioneer TV Western was the only program the network had in the top 15 shows (it held the #7 spot). During its mid–1950s heyday, an estimated 30,000,000 viewers tuned in for each week's episode (and a 65,000,000 viewership may have even occurred during its run).

Also working closely with Trendle and Chertok on the new series was writer Fran Striker. All three had been at the initial meeting in 1949 when Clayton Moore was interviewed for the title role.

Moore, who knew Chertok from MGM where both men had worked, recalled in his autobiography that discussion of the Lone Ranger "barely came up." The factors that won him the role of a lifetime were his athleticism and his having played the title role in *Ghost of Zorro*, a 1949 Republic serial.

The 1949 serial *Ghost of Zorro* with Clayton Moore (pictured) was a contributing factor when Moore won the Lone Ranger role.

Born in 1914, Jack Carlton Moore was a member of his high school gymnastics team. He was later a trapeze artist with an act called the Flying Behrs; in 1934, they performed at the Chicago World's Fair. He made his way to Hollywood in 1938, becoming both a stuntman and bit player. For Edward Small Productions, Moore had a strong supporting role in the 1940 Western feature *Kit Carson*. Small had him change his first name to Clayton.

Working with director William Witney also helped his acting career along. They first worked together in 1942 on the Western feature *Outlaws of Pine Ridge* and on Clayton's first Republic serial, *Perils of Nyoka*. Moore appeared in six Republic serials (he became known as the King of the Serials) prior to doing TV's *Lone Ranger*. As the Masked Rider of the Plains, the actor appeared in 169 of the 221 TV episodes.

Although it has been printed many times that Moore demanded more money after completing 78 episodes and two seasons as the Ranger (his salary was $500 per episode), he actually denied this in his autobiography. He stated that he never was informed why George Trendle and Jack Chertok had John Hart take over the title role for the third season of new productions (52 episodes).

Clayton Moore was initially seen as the Lone Ranger wearing a mask that did not cover his nose. As time passed, he was given one that did. After he was replaced, Moore felt it might have been the reason for the new mask. With Hart's mask also covering his nose, it apparently made it a bit harder to distinguish the two faces.

Hart's Ranger was taller than Moore's. This was especially noticeable when standing beside Jay Silverheels. Although he also cut a splendid figure as the Ranger, Hart lacked Moore's physical grace and charisma. Trendle and Chertok then put their original TV Ranger back into the saddle.

John Hart's first major starring role came in a Columbia serial for producer Sam Katzman: 1947's *Jack Armstrong—The All American Boy*. In 1954, he was seen in a serial starring Clayton Moore, *Gunfighters of the North West*. Prior to his stint as the Lone Ranger, Hart appeared as a bad guy in a couple of 1950 episodes of the series, "Rifles and Renegades" and "Sheriff of Gunstock." In 1957 he starred in 39 episodes of another Western series for syndicated television, *Hawkeye and the Last of the Mohicans*. This series was based on the classic James Fenimore Cooper novel *The Last of the Mohicans*. While Hart's character was

Seen without his mask in this *Ghost of Zorro* scene are Clayton Moore with Pamela Blake.

named Nat "Hawkeye" Cutler rather than the author's Natty Bumppo, his Indian sidekick, played by Lon Chaney, Jr., retained the name Chingachgook from the novel. There are obvious parallels with these noble characters and their counterparts the Lone Ranger and Tonto.

Moore and Hart had good things to say in later years about their friend and colleague Jay Silverheels. Born in 1918 as Harold J. Smith on the Six Nations Reservation in Canada, he was an authentic Mohawk Indian (the character Tonto was first identified on radio as being part of the Potawatomi tribe). The tribal name of Silverheels was given to him by an elder during his youth.

Jay and Clayton were first introduced when they became part of *The Lone Ranger* in 1949. Yet earlier that same year they appeared together in a Gene Autry Western, *The Cowboy and the Indians.*

Like Moore, Silverheels began his film career as a stuntman and was also an athlete, having competed as a boxer and in lacrosse. While

John Hart, an often overlooked Lone Ranger, played the role for one season.

the two men could kid each other about Tonto's broken English during the series, the friendship between the Ranger and his Indian companion, like their very own, was based on respect.

Silverheels was especially proud of portraying the great Apache Geronimo in three films: *Broken Arrow* in 1950, *Battle at Apache Pass* in 1952 and *Walk the Proud Land* in 1956. He spoke earnestly for the interests of all Native Americans in the film and TV industry.

There may have been some resentment on the actor's part in the 1960s with what he felt was Tonto's subordinate role. While it is true that the Lone Ranger gave the orders, both men were given many heroic moments; they were true compadres who could be called upon at any time to save the other from harm. Moore, Silverheels and Hart can be proud of their contribution to the series as enduring symbols of courage, fair play and loyalty for both youngsters and adults everywhere.

Silverheels and Moore were honored with their own stars on the Hollywood Walk of Fame. Jay's in 1979 was as the first American Indian to be so recognized. Clayton's in 1987 had both his own name and the Lone Ranger's name on it. Jay appeared in 217 episodes of the TV series, missing four due to a heart attack in 1954. Over the years they made many personal appearances in character for their legions of fans.

A tremendous cast of guest stars helped to make the series special. Seen in the recurring role of the Ranger's nephew Dan Reid, Jr., was Chuck Courtney. Born in 1930, he was 20 when Dan was introduced in episode #22, "Sheep Thieves," The engaging actor played the character in 14 episodes between 1950 and 1955; the last was "The Swami."

Two of the episodes included Dan's name in the title: "Dan Reid's Fight for Life" and "Dan Reid's Sacrifice." The latter featured his own trusted horse Victor in the story. The steed nicely complimented the Lone Ranger Silver and Tonto's Scout. In fact, Silver was the father.

During the 1960s, Courtney was a guest star on eight episodes of the TV series *The Virginian*, playing different roles. He was also part of the cast of a couple of John Wayne's later Westerns, *Rio Lobo* (1970) and *The Cowboys* (1972). He died in January 2000, at age 69.

Playing Captain Reid, Dan's father, on the first episode of the series was Tristram Coffin. Coffin appeared as various characters on a total of five episodes of the series between 1949 and 1957. By the time he did his last one, "Canuck," the actor had shortened his first name to Tris.

Born in 1909, Coffin amassed hundreds of film and TV credits. He was in Moore's earlier *Perils of Nyoka*; and he was a guest star on nine episodes of the popular *Cisco Kid* TV series of the 1950s. Coffin's final TV Western credits were eight episodes of *Death Valley Days* between 1965 and 1970. He was 80 when he died in 1990.

At least five future TV Western stars guest starred on *The Lone Ranger*. James Arness, Marshal Matt Dillon on *Gunsmoke*, was a deputy in episode #33, "A Matter of Courage." Matt's deputy Chester was played by Dennis Weaver, who was in #162, "The Tell-Tale Bullet." Robert Horton, scout Flint McCullough on *Wagon Train*, was in #142,

"Tenderfoot." Guy Williams, the star of *Zorro*, was seen in #172, "Six-Gun Artist."

My favorite, Gall Davis, graced four episodes of the series: #25, "Buried Treasure," #38, "Spanish Gold," #77, "Friend in Need," and #89, "Trial by Fire." As Betty Jeanne Grayson, she was born in 1925. She appeared in 15 episodes of *The Gene Autry Show* from 1951 to 1954; he called her the "perfect Western actress." Her real claim to fame was her very own series, *Annie Oakley* (81 episodes between 1954 and 1957). In 1959, the actress made a cameo appearance as Annie Oakley in Bob Hope's comedy Western *Alias Jesse James*. She and Jay Silverheels (as Tonto) were among a number of stars who came to the comedian's rescue against the bad guys. Davis was 71 when she passed away in 1997.

Appearing in more *Lone Ranger* episodes than any other actress was Nan Leslie. Her eight were between 1949 and 1955. The lovely Nanette June Leslie (1926–2000) was at RKO in 1945 when she met Gail Davis and they became close friends. She appeared in a 1954 episode of Gail's *Annie Oakley* series. In the 1950s, Nan also guest starred on *The Cisco Kid* and *The Adventures of Kit Carson* (five episodes each). In the 1957–58 TV season, she played Martha McGivern in 37 episodes of another Western series, *The Californians*.

Other easily recognizable performers from TV Westerns of the 1950s and 1960s appeared on *The Lone Ranger*. Johnny Crawford and Paul Fix, regulars on the popular series *The Rifleman*, were each on one episode. So were Lee Aaker and James Brown, the stars of *The Adventures of Rin Tin Tin*, another popular show. Jack Elam, a regular on the lesser known *The Dakotas*, was in two *Ranger* episodes. One of the best bad guys, often with wild abandon, on both film and television, Elam also played good guys quite well. He had a knack for conveying humor in both instances.

William Fawcett, who played Pete on *Fury*, was in five *Lone Ranger* episodes; Ray Teal, Sheriff Coffee on *Bonanza*, was in four. Gene Evans, the father on *My Friend Flicka*, was in three.

Martin Milner and DeForest Kelley, who played Burt Lancaster's brothers in *Gunfight at the O.K. Corral* (1957), were seen in back-to-back episodes in the first season: Kelley was in #27 "Gold Train," and Milner was in #28 "Pay Dirt." Kelley ended up in three *Ranger* episodes.

Many would call John Ford the best of all Western film directors.

Some of the players he used were also featured in *Lone Ranger* episodes; and this included his own brother, Francis Ford, in a 1950 episode. Harry Carey, Jr., who played a starring role in Ford's *Three Godfathers* (1948), appeared in episode #174 "Return of Dice Dawson."

Hank Worden played Mose Harper in one of Ford's greatest Westerns, 1956's *The Searchers*; Worden appeared in six *Ranger* episodes between 1949 and 1957. Another of my favorite John Ford movie characters was Clementine Carter, played by the exquisite Cathy Downs in 1946's equally great *My Darling Clementine*. She was seen in a 1953 episode, "Best Laid Plans."

While Ford's *Stagecoach* made a star of John Wayne in 1939, it also had a memorable villain, Luke Plummer. This bad guy was played by Tom Tyler. During the 1940s, Tyler was notable for his good guys as well. One of them was another masked hero, the Phantom, in a serial of the same name. Tyler appeared in one *Lone Ranger* episode in 1950, "Damsels in Distress."

On *The Lone Ranger*, good always triumphed over evil in the end. It all began in 1949 with a three-episode arc directed by George Seitz. It introduced a new Lone Ranger to TV viewers and brought his nemesis Butch Cavendish to justice.

Glenn Strange brought his formidable stature into play for the first three shows as the dastardly Cavendish. The actor returned in the role in a 1950 episode with Moore, "Never Say Die," and with Hart in a 1953 episode, "Gunpowder Joe." Strange appeared in three more episodes in other roles, bringing his total to eight between 1949 and 1955. His final episode was "The Too-Perfect Signature."

Born in 1922, Lane Bradford was still a teenager when he began his acting career in 1940s "B" Westerns. Before long, he was riding the same outlaw trail as his father, actor John Merton, one of the main villains from the 1938 *Lone Ranger* serial. John LeVarre, Sr., and John LeVarre, Jr., were their actual names.

While Merton was in three episodes of the TV series between 1949 and 1953, his son was a guest star on the most. Between 1949 and 1957, he appeared in 15 episodes; with the first being #4, "The Legion of Old Timers," and the last #216, "Mission for Tonto." Bradford first worked with Clayton Moore in the 1948 serial *Adventures of Frank and Jesse James*. They were together a decade later for *The Lone Ranger and the Lost City of Gold.*

Certainly one of the most recognized and toughest TV Westerns bad guys, Bradford's credits included *Annie Oakley* (eight episodes), *Gunsmoke* and *Bonanza* (over a dozen each). When you saw him around, you knew the good guys had better watch out. The actor was only 50 when he died from a cerebral hemorrhage in June 1973.

Hollywood legend has it that actor John Doucette was the fastest with a six-gun. He was not tall like Lane Bradford and Glenn Strange, but his stocky frame and deep voice made him just as menacing a bad guy. My favorite Doucette character was his decent, good-natured undertaker in the 1965 John Wayne Western *The Sons of Katie Elder*.

Doucette, born in 1921, began his acting career during the 1940s. He and Clayton Moore were both in the 1949 "B" Western *Bandits of El Dorado* with Charles Starrett as the hero. That same year, Doucette made his first *Lone Ranger* episode, "The Masked Rider." Ten more followed, all in different roles, the last being 1955's "Counterfeit Redskins."

Other early TV Western credits for Doucette included the popular *Gene Autry* and *Roy Rogers* shows. During the 1960s, he was in eight episodes of another top series, *Wagon Train*. In 1994, he died at 73.

James Griffith's tall, thin frame was seen to good advantage in many TV episodes and films. Sometimes he played a good guy but more often it was a heavy. Born in 1916, his initial work on TV Westerns was on *The Gene Autry Show* and *The Lone Ranger* in 1950. He appeared on a total of seven *Ranger* episodes, with his last, "A Message from Abe." In this one, he steals money from his father-in-law, but only to save the life of his wife. It is one of my favorite episodes.

The actor also acted on other Western series in the 1950s: *Trackdown* as a barber and *Sheriff of Cochise* as a deputy. In the 1959–60 TV season, the latter show was retitled *U.S. Marshal* and Griffith continued playing his role. He was 77 when he died in September 1993.

Myron Healey appeared in seven *Lone Ranger* shows in various roles. Three of those were in the last eight episodes of the series, Healey's final one being "Blind Witness." Born in 1923, he was still in his twenties when he began working on TV Westerns in the 1950s. Becoming one of the most recognized heavies, he was ranked right up there with Lane Bradford.

Among the actor's many TV roles were portrayals of actual Old West bad men: outlaw Bob Dalton in a 1954 episode of *Stories of the*

Century and gunfighter Johnny Ringo in a 1958 *Tombstone Territory*. In the 1958–59 season of *The Life and Legend of Wyatt Earp*, Healey had the regular role of gunman Doc Holliday.

But Healey's stern, handsome features served him well too as a good guy. He was chief aide to Leslie Nielsen's Swamp Fox on seven episodes of the *Walt Disney* series between 1959 and 1961. In 2005, he died at age 82.

Harry Lauter, like Healey, was a tall, handsome actor adept at playing heavies in TV Westerns. I especially remember him for his heroic turn in a 1950s series called *Tales of the Texas Rangers*. He played Ranger Clay Morgan in some 52 episodes. He was born Herman Arthur Lauter in 1914. His first *Lone Ranger* episode was 1949's "Rustler's Hideout." Ten more featured the actor in various roles; the last was 1956's "Ghost Canyon." A dozen episodes of both *Annie Oakley* and *Rawhide* benefited from his strong presence. He also appeared in a few episodes of another 1960s show, and one of my favorites, *The Wild Wild West*. At age 76, Lauter died in 1990 of heart failure.

Two performers who appeared as *Lone Ranger* characters on the wrong side of the law became known for their wonderful roles on other hit TV shows: Frances Bavier and George J. Lewis. She played Bee Taylor, the beloved aunt, on *The Andy Griffith Show* (1960–68) and *Mayberry R.F.D.* (1968–70), and Lewis played Don Alejandro de la Vega, the hero's father, on *Zorro* (1957–59) and *Walt Disney* (1960–61).

Frances only appeared on one *Ranger* episode but it was a humdinger: "Sawtelle Saga's End" in 1955. The actress played another aunt, Maggie Sawtelle, but this one was the leader of a gang of bank robbers.

Seen in the initial two episodes of the *Ranger* series, Lewis was Collins, who betrays the Texas Rangers to the Cavendish gang. The actor later appeared on three other episodes but in different roles.

At least 450 guest stars appeared on the *Lone Ranger* show between 1949 and 1957. Also included were such familiar names as Hugh Beaumont, Rand Brooks, Richard Crane, Beverly Garland, Martha Hyer, Marjorie Lord, Slim Pickens, Denver Pyle, Craig Stevens and Lee Van Cleef. Film and TV buffs will remember them all.

Eight men were responsible for directing the performers in the 221 episodes. They were George Seitz, Jr., George Archainbaud, John

H. Morse, Paul Landres, William J. Thiele, Oscar Rudolph, Earl Bellamy and Charles D. Livingstone.

Seitz directed a total of 43 *Lone Ranger* episodes between 1949 and 1951. After the first nine in a row to begin the series, he directed 21 more during that initial season. In the second season, he directed 13. Five episodes that Seitz directed (#1, 2, 3, 27 and 34) were also written by him. He also wrote the 1953 episode "Gentleman from Julesburg," which was directed by Paul Landres.

Born in 1915, George Seitz, Jr., had a short career in film and TV. (His father George Seitz, had an extensive list of directing credits including the popular Andy Hardy series in the 1940s.) Seitz Jr. died at 87 in 2002.

Following Seitz, Jr., as director on the tenth *Ranger* episode, "High Heels," was George Archainbaud. He went on to direct a total of 14 shows in the first season. Archainbaud was born in 1890 and his film career started as an assistant director and then director on silent pictures. Among his later Western features was a 1943 Hopalong Cassidy adventure, *Hoppy Serves a Writ*. He also directed 26 episodes of the *Cassidy* TV series between 1952 and 1954. He directed 47 of Gene Autry's TV episodes during the 1950s. All set to be a full-time director on Rory Calhoun's TV series *The Texan*—he had already directed one episode—he died in February 1959, at 68.

Directing more *Lone Ranger* shows than anyone else was John H. Morse. Fifty were to his credit between 1950 and 1953. Beginning with #39, "Damsels in Distress," he directed eight of that first season's 52 episodes; 13 of the second's 26 shows; and 29 of the third's 52 episodes. His final one was #130, "The Red Mark."

He was born John Hollingsworth Morse in 1910, and it appears that he only used his first name early in his television directing career, on the *Ranger* series and 15 episodes of *Sky King*. After that, he was billed as Hollingsworth Morse. He helmed 58 episodes of *Lassie* between 1959 and 1964 and 46 episodes of *McHale's Navy* from 1964 to 1966. Morse died at age 77 in 1988.

Paul Landres' initial episode was #79, "Outlaw's Son," his last one #127, "Old Bailey." He directed a total of 23 episodes. Born in 1912, Landres began a film career in 1931 as an assistant editor. In 1949 he started directing "B" Westerns. His list of TV credits was quite extensive. During the 1950s, he directed 31 episodes of *The Cisco Kid* and

25 of *The Life and Legend of Wyatt Earp*. He also directed a few episodes of another of my favorites, *Daniel Boone*. In 2001, the director died at age 89.

Wilhelm Isersohn was born in 1890 and, as William Thiele, directed Johnny Weissmuller *in Tarzan Triumphs* and *Tarzan's Desert Mystery* in 1943. Thiele included the middle initial J. in his name for his work on *The Lone Ranger*. In the 1954–55 season, he directed 26 episodes. The initial one was the season opener "The Fugitive." The director had started his career making German films in the 1920s. He then pursued a career in America, the name change coming in 1936. He also directed a 1956 episode of *Broken Arrow*. He died at 85 in 1975.

Of the 52 episodes in the fourth season, Oscar Rudolph directed 22. He also directed ten episodes in the fifth and final season; his last one, "Outlaws in Grease Paint," was the 221st and last episode in the series. During his career, Rudolph (1911–1991) accumulated a long list of TV credits. Along with his 32 *Lone Rangers*, he directed 50 episodes of *The Donna Reed Show* between 1958 and 1960. Rudolph seemed especially attuned to comedy-flavored shows like the *Reed* series. They also included 37 *Batman* episodes and 27 *Brady Bunch* episodes.

Earl Bellamy directed 29 out of 39 episodes in the 1956–57 season. Born in 1917, he began his career as an assistant director in 1939. But it was as a TV director that Bellamy made his mark. Over 1600 series episodes were helmed by him between 1954 and 1985. On another Western series of the 1950s, *Tales of Wells Fargo*, he directed 42 episodes. And on the 1950s comedy series *Bachelor Father*, he directed 82 episodes. He also directed 24 episodes of *My Three Sons* in the early 1970s. Bellamy died in 2003 at 86.

Directing only four *Lone Rangers* was Charles D. Livingstone. He was born in 1903 and originally started out on the *Lone Ranger* radio series playing heavies. He even played the villain in a brief *Lone Ranger* stage production in the Detroit area a year or so after his 1933 start on radio. In early 1954, George Trendle asked Livingstone, who had directed the radio series for over 15 years at that point, to help coordinate the TV show. He agreed with the stipulation that he would also direct some of the episodes. Livingstone passed away in 1986 at 83.

Clayton Moore played the Lone Ranger for the first two TV seasons, and was replaced by John Hart for the third. In June 1954, Moore was rehired. Just as he never knew the reason he was fired, he was not informed why Hart was let go. Moore wrote in his autobiography that fans told him that Hart "did a creditable job, but that they could just never accept him as the real Lone Ranger."

As Moore was being rehired, George Trendle was negotiating with Jack Wrather to buy all rights to the Lone Ranger. The last live radio show aired just six days before Moore's return for the fourth season's opening episode on September 9, 1954. By then, Wrather had purchased all rights for $3,000,000.

After 182 TV episodes, both Jack Chertok and associate producer Harry Poppe left the series, having worked for both Trendle and Wrather. Poppe's son Harry Jr. worked as a writer on the series between 1949 and 1955, also for both owners. Among the new people who joined Wrather was producer Sherman A. Harris for the final season. Harris produced the 1958 feature film as well.

Still heard on the show after the changeover was the famous opening introduction by announcer Fred Foy and closing "Hi-Yo, Silver! Away!" by Earle Graser. Foy also did most of the announcing on the series, although film and TV actor Gerald Mohr functioned too as narrator on the initial 18 episodes. Also in the show's final season under Wrather, all 39 of its episodes were shot in color (the previous ones were black and white).

John Devereaux Wrather, Jr., born in 1918, made his fortune beside his father in the oil business. An entrepreneur like Trendle, he began producing films in 1946. But it was on TV that he became more widely known. In addition to acquiring *The Lone Ranger* in 1954, Wrather also began the long-running *Lassie* TV series. Clayton Moore appeared in costume as the Ranger in the 1959 *Lassie* episode "Peace Patrol."

Jack Wrather Productions were also behind the *Ranger* films in 1956 and 1958. Another TV series that Wrather made popular in the 1950s was *Sergeant Preston of the Yukon*. It was derived from *Challenge of the Yukon*, a Trendle radio show which first aired in 1938.

In the beginning of each *Lone Ranger* episode, the Masked Man is seen galloping on Silver, his majestic steed. He then rears up the horse on its hind legs for a spectacular shot with an unique and towering rock formation in the background. Called Lone Ranger Rock, it's located in Chatsworth, California, near Iverson's Ranch where many Westerns were made. Although civilization would bring condominiums and a highway to the area, Moore fondly remembered it as "wild, beautiful country."

The rider performing the scene at Lone Ranger Rock was actually Moore on Silver #1. The actor had helped acquire the horse from Hugh Hooker's ranch in California's San Fernando Valley. The stallion was affectionately nicknamed "Liver Lip" on the set because he moved his tongue across the roller on the bit, making the lower lip protrude.

When John Hart played the Ranger, a second horse was brought in (Moore later used it too). The difference between the two stallions was that the first one had a dark spot on the backside, which was dyed white for filming, and the second one had a small dark spot on its left ear. Clayton used the second steed for his personal appearances.

Another popular location for filming *The Lone Ranger* was located in the foothills of the Santa Susana Mountains. Used for other Westerns as well, this one, the Corriganville Movie Ranch, was located in Simi Valley. It was owned by "B" Western star Ray "Crash" Corrigan. Still another great location for Westerns (including *The Lone Ranger*) was the Melody Ranch Motion Picture Studio in Santa Clarita Valley, California. It was acquired in 1952 by Gene Autry.

All three places—Iverson's, Corriganville and Melody Ranch—had terrific terrain for making Westerns, and their own Western streets as well. While the Iverson Ranch, owned by brothers Joseph and Aaron Iverson, was the main location for the show's first season, Hollywood's Bronson Canyon was used for the first episode where Cavendish and his outlaws ambush the Texas Rangers.

During the Trendle years on the series, interiors were filmed at the Hal Roach Studios in Culver City, California. This was where those delightful Laurel and Hardy comedy shorts of the 1930s were made. A Western street was set up there too.

Under Jack Wrather, interiors were shot at General Service Studio. There was also a Western street at this studio.

The Lone Ranger was a relatively low-budget TV series sponsored by General Mills, famous for its breakfast cereals. In 1949, the budget for each episode was set at $12,500. Sometimes location work included picking up shots for future episodes; and sometimes those shots were reused in different episodes. Budgets improved over the years so by 1954, under Wrather, each episode had an $18,000 budget.

After Wrather took over the Ranger franchise, a TV special was seen on February 12, 1955: *The Lone Ranger Rides Again* was a one-hour version of the original three episodes of the series. I found a DVD of a somewhat longer feature version of these three episodes, titled *The Legend of the Lone Ranger.*

Of particular interest in these edited treatments is the Lone Ranger's origin, taken from the Fran Striker radio story. Both the Texas Rangers ambush in the canyon and Tonto finding the lone survivor are included. Yet also shared was Silver's rescue from the buffalo attack; and the Ranger's silver mine, his source of income and bullets, entrusted to the care of old-timer Jim Blaine.

Also of interest for Lone Ranger fans was that he only used a single holster and gun on the three initial shows. In all subsequent episodes, he wears the double-holstered gun belt.

There are actually many DVDs available on various *Lone Ranger* television episodes. In fact, every one of the 221 episodes of the series was included in a 30-disc set in June 2013 by Classic Media.

The Nielsen TV ratings did not officially begin until the 1950–51 season. *The Lone Ranger*'s #7 listing would prove to be the best one for the series as well. Only one other Western show (*Hopalong Cassidy* at #9) made it onto that season's listing of the top 25 shows.

During the 1951–52 TV season, *The Lone Ranger* was only seen in reruns but still placed #18 on the list of top prime time shows. In its actual third season of new shows, 1952–53, the show was #29 of the top 30 programs. No other Westerns were listed in those two seasons.

The Lone Ranger was not listed among the top 30 shows in its fourth and fifth seasons of new productions. Other Western series that would soon be making the list were *Gunsmoke* and *The Life and Legend of Wyatt Earp*. Both shows represented the more adult TV Westerns coming into vogue. While *The Lone Ranger* without a doubt was enjoyed by adults too, it was considered more of a children's show.

The series was nominated for an Emmy Award as Best Children's Show of 1950. *Time for Beany* was the winner, with *The Cisco Kid* as the runner-up.

In its debut year, 1949, *The Lone Ranger* was the runner-up as Best Film Made For and Viewed on Television. *Life of Riley* won the Emmy in that category.

For the 2005 TV Land Awards, Clayton Moore was nominated as Favorite Crimestopper. When the radio show debuted on radio in 1933,

Moore was 18 years old. He remembered listening to the later Brace Beemer shows and enjoying them with his father. Little did he know that one day he would be playing the Lone Ranger, the one we remember more than any other.

The United States Postal Service honored *The Lone Ranger* in August 2009, with Clayton Moore and Silver appearing on postage stamps. Twenty television shows were honored; others were *I Love Lucy, Lassie* and *Hopalong Cassidy*. They were all part of a series of stamps called Early TV Memories.

Six

The 1956 Film
The Lone Ranger

Don't worry about this mask. It's on the side of the law.
—The Lone Ranger to young Pete Ramirez

Released by Warner Brothers Presentation. A Jack Wrather Production. New York City Premiere: February 10, 1956. Released on February 25, 1956. 86 minutes. WarnerColor.

Credits:
Producer: Willis Goldbeck.
Director: Stuart Heisler.
Screenplay: Herb Meadow.
Photography: Edwin B. DuPar.
Editor: Clarence Kolster.
Art Director: Stanley Fleischer.
Set Decorator: G.W. Berntsen.
Makeup: Gordon Bau.
Wardrobe: Peg McKeon, Gene J. Martin.
Music: David Buttolph.

Cast:
Clayton Moore (The Lone Ranger); Jay Silverheels (Tonto); Lyle Bettger (Reece Kilgore); Bonita Granville (Welcome Kilgore); Perry Lopez (Pete Ramirez); Robert Wilke (Cassidy); John Pickard (Sheriff Sam Kimberley); Beverly Washburn (Lila Kilgore); Michael Ansara (Angry Horse); Frank de Kova (Chief Red Hawk); Charles Meredith (Governor); Mickey Simpson (Powder); Zon Murray (Goss); Lane Chandler (Whitebeard); Lee Roberts (John Muller); Edward Colmans (Padre); William Schallert (Clive); Hank Patterson (Old Man Kimberley); Malcolm Atterbury (Phineas Tripp).

Synopsis: When a small band of Indians chase after a rider, the Lone Ranger and Tonto come to his rescue. The rider, Pete Ramirez, has lost his small herd of cattle to the Indians.

The territorial governor arrives at the Kilgore ranch with great fanfare. It is owned by Reece Kilgore, who resides there with his wife Welcome and their daughter Lila. There is apparent tension in the marriage, especially over the raising of the child. Kilgore's employees include Cassidy the foreman, Powder and Goss.

Aware that Kilgore wants to remove the Indians from their reservation land, the governor seeks counsel from the Lone Ranger at a nearby mission church. The Ranger is at first disguised as an old prospector in order to discern the governor's true character. This done, the Masked Man reveals his identity.

Tonto and the Ranger go onto the Indian reservation and ask their friend Chief Red Hawk about Indian arrows found in cattle. The old chief denies any wrongdoing, but still feels a last fight with the settlers may be inevitable. This is due to the encroachment upon Indian land, including the sacred Spirit Mountain.

In the town of Brasada, Cassidy rounds up men, including young Ramirez, for a cattle drive to Abilene. An argument arises between the Kilgore foreman and Sheriff Kimberley over trespassing on the reservation. The Lone Ranger, in his prospector guise, amusingly keeps a fight from breaking out between the two men.

At the Kilgore ranch, Kilgore shows pride in little Lila and even plans on having her take over the spread one day. But her mother always worries about her being in danger.

Pete Ramirez is alerted by the Lone Ranger to watch for anything suspicious on the drive. While trying to recover his steers from the Kilgore herd, the sheriff's father is shot down by Cassidy. Ramirez did not see the shooting but suspects foul play. In Abilene, Ramirez learns that Kilgore wants dynamite brought back to the ranch. The young man is killed by Cassidy for snooping.

Back with Kilgore in Brasada, Cassidy claims Ramirez ran off and that Indians killed the sheriff's father. When Kilgore and Cassidy spot Tonto, they think he is from the reservation and a mob is incited to hang him. The Lone Ranger saves his friend in the nick of time.

Investigating Ramirez's disappearance in Abilene, the Ranger again uses his prospector's disguise. He learns not only of the man's death but about the dynamite.

On the reservation, the Ranger and Tonto find Red Hawk's tribe preparing for war. There is a heated dispute between the Masked Man and Angry Horse, a young warrior who wants to be the new chief.

When Indians are found burning crops, Tonto and the Ranger bring them before Sheriff Kimberley. These "Indians" are revealed to be white men in disguise and they work for Kilgore. The sheriff agrees to help the Lone Ranger by going to the governor.

With an Indian uprising coming, one that he started, Kilgore sends his daughter to a safer place. But she is captured by Red Hawk's Indians. The Lone Ranger and Angry Horse fight over her, and the Ranger brings the child safely home to her mother.

The Ranger learns from Welcome that Spirit Mountain is being dynamited by her husband. In a mountain tunnel, Kilgore kills his own man Goss in a dispute. Finding Kilgore and his other henchmen there, the Lone Ranger is forced to shoot Powder but is injured by Cassidy.

While the Ranger's injury is not serious, he is weakened by a fall down a steep hill. He is helped by both his horse Silver and Tonto. The Masked Man and his Indian companion then discover the reason for the dynamite is a silver lode.

As Kilgore, Cassidy and settlers ride against the Indians, and the Indians move against them, Tonto and the Lone Ranger hold them at bay. They do so using the dynamite. The sheriff, now a U.S. marshal, arrives with the cavalry to stop the impending conflict. Kilgore denies having had a hand in the Ramirez killing, but he is shot dead by Cassidy. Trying to escape, Cassidy is chased by the Lone Ranger and apprehended.

Before riding away, Tonto and the Lone Ranger visit Welcome and Lila at the mission. Both mother and daughter will be staying on at the ranch now that the territory is a safe place to live.

"Thunders to the Motion Picture Screen!" proclaimed the ads for the first Lone Ranger production in color. It was released by Warner Brothers in early 1956, when the final season of the TV series was months away—it would also be in color.

A striking ad for the 1956 feature film *The Lone Ranger*.

Jack Wrather's production company was behind this exciting film. After Clayton Moore began the fourth season of new TV episodes, it was under Wrather who had then recently taken over the show and all rights to the Western hero from George W. Trendle. Wrather had asked Moore's input, and the actor mentioned the larger mask that became visible prior to initial release from the series in 1952. Clayton shared with Jack Wrather his feelings about returning to the smaller mask so as to make the Ranger not seem like an outlaw. And that easily, it was done.

Wrather's wife was actress Bonita Granville, who played Welcome Kilgore in the feature film. "She was a lovely person, easy to work with, and talented," said Clayton. The Wrathers were married in 1947. Bonita had made her mark in films as a child actress. Born in 1923, she was only 13 when she received an Oscar nomination as Best Supporting Actress for *These Three* in 1936. She also appeared in the title role in a series of Nancy Drew mystery films in 1938 and 1939. The *Lone Ranger* feature would prove to be her last film as an actress. But for many years she was the producer of the *Lassie* TV series for her husband's company. Like Clayton Moore and Jay Silverheels, she has a star on the Hollywood Walk of Fame. Bonita Granville Wrather died of lung cancer at age 65 in 1988. Her 66-year-old husband had died of cancer in 1984.

The camaraderie between Silverheels' Tonto and Moore's Ranger lights up the screen when they are first seen together at the start of the film. Sitting atop a hillside on Scout and Silver, they do not even have to say anything to each other. They need only to share a smile for the magic between the two characters to register.

Producer Willis Goldbeck, director Stuart Heisler and screenwriter Herb Meadow were faithful to the Lone Ranger legend. Early in the story we see the Masked Man relating his past to Charles Meredith's governor in an inspiring scene.

Appearing in this same sequence is Clayton Moore's old geezer of a prospector, bowlegged and funny, who popped up on the television series. The actor also appeared in disguise in other roles on the series and always with great versatility. John Hart did the same but without the same gusto.

Willis Goldbeck was quite versatile in his own right. He actually started out in the film business as a screenwriter in the 1920s. One of his much later screenplays, and one of my favorite Westerns, was *The Man Who Shot Liberty Valance* (1962). He also produced and John Ford directed that classic.

For Burt Lancaster's 1951 adventure *Ten Tall Men*, Goldbeck directed and contributed to the story. He may be best remembered for his work on the popular *Dr. Kildare* films of the 1930s and 1940s. He was involved as a writer on most of them, and directed some too.

Liberty Valance was Goldbeck's last film before he retired. He died at age 80 in 1977.

Stuart Heisler (1896–1979) began his film career as a prop man in 1913. In 1940 he became a director with *The Biscuit Eater,* about a boy and his dog. Heisler directed Susan Hayward and Bette Davis in films for which they were Oscar-nominated as Best Actress. Hayward's nomination was in 1947's *Smash Up: The Story of a Woman,* Davis' for 1952's *The Star.* Moving into television, Heisler directed a number of Western shows, including 27 episodes of *Lawman.* In 1963, the year before his retirement, he worked on eight episodes of *The Dakotas.*

Prior to his *Lone Ranger* film storyline, Herb Meadow also wrote ten 10 episodes of the series. He was born in 1911 as Herman Meadow and entered the world of series TV via the *Lone Ranger* show. He went on to create the *Have Gun, Will Travel* series in 1957. When that Western left the air in 1963, Meadow developed the drama series *Arrest and Trial.* He later wrote for *The Virginian* (one episode in 1966, another in 1969). Meadow was 83 when he passed away in 1995.

Reviewing *The Lone Ranger* in its April 1956 issue, *National Parent-Teacher* magazine opined, "The story has the ingredients of all good Westerns, a cattle stampede, Indians on the warpath, a sneering bad man, an abundance of cliffs to fall from and ride over, and, of course, a hero."

This Western has a fine ensemble of supporting players to shine right alongside our two main heroes. Pete Ramirez (played by Perry Lopez) has youth, ambition and a girl he loves when he is cut down in the prime of his life. Conveyed strongly by the actor were the character's pride and decency. Born in 1929, Lopez was just 26 when the film was made in August and September 1955. During the 1950s, he appeared in a few Alan Ladd films, including a 1954 Western called *Drum Beat* which I enjoyed. I also remember him as the younger brother of Tony Curtis in the 1962 adventure *Taras Bulba.* Lopez had a recurring role in 1958 on the *Zorro* series.

Perhaps most film buffs will remember the actor for his work alongside Jack Nicholson in 1974's *Chinatown* and its 1990 sequel *The Two Jakes.* Lung cancer took the life of Perry Lopez in 2008 when he was 78.

Clayton Moore and Jay Silverheels on Scout confront Perry Lopez in this scene from 1956's *The Lone Ranger*.

The fate of Pete Ramirez might have been different if he had heeded Sheriff Kimberley and became his deputy. John Pickard played the stalwart lawman, who briefly lost his way but not his life in coming to grips with his duties. Pickard, who was born in 1913, appeared in assorted roles in seven *Lone Ranger* TV episodes between 1952 and 1957, including the final episode "Outlaws in Greasepaint." During the 1950s, he was in Jack Wrather's other two shows as well—*Sergeant Preston of the Yukon*, on four episodes, and three on *Lassie*.

A stern fortitude as an actor seemed especially suitable for portraying military men and lawmen. Such was the case for Pickard not only in the *Lone Ranger* film, but with recurring television roles as a sergeant major in 1961's *Gunslinger* and in the 1970s as a colonel on *How the West Was Won*. In 1955, Pickard almost won the role of Marshal Dillon on *Gunsmoke*. He did appear in various roles on 12 episodes of the series between 1960 and 1975. Tragically, in August 1993 at age 80, he was killed on a farm by a bull.

Like Pickard's lawman, Charles Meredith as the kindly yet authoritative territorial governor accepts a guiding hand from the Lone Ranger. Born in 1894, Meredith started out acting in silent pictures. His first television work was on *The Lone Ranger*: Between 1948 and 1955, he played doctors in "Cannonball McKay," "Message to Fort Apache" and "The Too-Perfect Signature." He was again seen as a territorial governor on a 1959 episode of *Lawman*. Meredith played many doctors, reverends and political figures over a long career. His last role was as a reverend in a 1964 Audie Murphy Western, *The Quick Gun*. In November of that year, he died at age 70.

Born in 1910, Frank de Kova gave up a teaching career to become an actor. His flair for playing menacing figures was on display in 1952's *Viva Zapata*, as the treacherous colonel who plots the title character's death. In 1959, *Westinghouse Desilu Playhouse* introduced the TV series *The Untouchables* with a two-parter in which de Kova was a hit man out to get hero Eliot Ness.

It was in Indian roles that the actor made his mark. Along with his wise and sympathetic chief in *The Lone Ranger*, he played Native Americans on many TV shows, including seven episodes of *Cheyenne* and eight of *Wagon Train*. Especially memorable was de Kova's colorful Chief Wild Eagle in 63 episodes of the wild Western comedy *F Troop* (1965–67). In 1981, he passed away at age 71.

De Kova's Chief Red Hawk is clearly moved by the Lone Ranger risking life and limb for the welfare of little Lila Kilgore. She was played by Beverly Washburn, one of the brightest young actresses of her day. She was born in 1943 and her acting career began in 1950. In 1953's *Shane*, she played Ruth Lewis, whose family's homestead is burned by the Rykers. Endearing, sweet-natured film performances followed in *The Lone Ranger* in 1956 and *Old Yeller* the following year.

On TV, Beverly was in a number of shows seen in my own childhood. They included episodes of *Father Knows Best* in 1957, *Shirley Temple's Storybook* in 1958, and *Leave It to Beaver* in 1957. Beverly may be remembered most of all for her association with a legendary Hollywood actress. Between 1954 and 1956, she appeared on three episodes of *The Loretta Young Show*, and in the 1962–63 TV season she played oldest daughter Vickie Massey on *The New Loretta Young Show.*

One of Beverly Washburn's first screen credits was as a young spectator enjoying the circus in 1952's *The Greatest Show on Earth.* Playing a prominent role as the villainous elephant handler in that film was Lyle Bettger (1915–2003), who was Beverly's father in *The Lone Ranger.* The only redeeming quality of Bettger's Reece Kilgore was the affection he had for his daughter. Otherwise, the character fit the mold of scheming, murderous bad guys the versatile actor was good at playing. He seemed especially adept at using his blond, handsome features and stately bearing as a cover for his unsavory characters. He gave another memorable performance as outlaw leader Ike Clanton in 1957's *Gunfight at the O.K. Corral.* Incidentally, brother Finn Clanton in this Western was played by Lee Roberts, Bettger's nemesis Indian agent John Muller in *The Lone Ranger.*

The actor was seen as good guys as well. While his rancher and Charles Meredith's governor were on opposite sides of the law in the 1956 film, they fought for the greater good as regular cast members on the TV series *The Court of Last Resort* (1957–58).

Possibly the greatest Western heavy of all time was Robert J. Wilke. Sometimes he left his middle initial (for Joseph) off his name, and sometimes he just used Bob as his first. He was born in 1914; during 1933 and 1934 he performed as a high diver at the Chicago's World Fair where Clayton Moore performed on the trapeze. One of Wilke's roles in the 1940s was in *The Crimson Ghost,* the 1946 serial with Moore's first appearance as a bad guy.

Some of Bob Wilke's first TV work in the early 1950s was on *The Gene Autry Show* and *The Lone Ranger.* In 1952's *High Noon,* the actor was one of the four gunmen out to get Gary Cooper. Western fans will never forget him putting his gun against a knife in 1960's *The Magnificent Seven.* As the cunning and vicious Cassidy in the *Lone Ranger* film, he gave one of his strongest performances. Wilke had over 300 film and television roles to his credit. In the 1950s and 1960s, Bob Wilke was seen on many different Western shows. He made the most appearances on *The Range Rider* (eight), and did seven each of *Gunsmoke* and *Laramie.* Once in a while, he was even seen as a good guy including his marshal in the 1971 film *A Gunfight.* Cancer was the cause of his death, at 74, in 1989.

Michael Ansara's aptly named Angry Horse made a formidable foe for Clayton Moore's masked man in the 1956 feature film *The Lone Ranger*.

Michael George Ansara was born in 1922. Before being cast as the aptly named Angry Horse in the feature film, the actor played other roles on two earlier *Lone Ranger* TV episodes, "Trouble at Black Rock" in 1951 and "Outlaw Underground" in 1952. Tall, with dark features and a powerful presence, Ansara portrayed both villains and heroes with equal aplomb.

Following his turn as the hateful Indian warrior in *The Lone Ranger*, he co-starred as the heroic Apache Cochise on the *Broken Arrow* TV series from 1956 to 1958. In 1959, a couple of appearances as upstanding Native American lawman Sam Buckhart on *The Rifleman* led to playing the role for a single season on another series, *Law of the Plainsman*.

Ansara played the Klingon villain Kang on three different *Star*

Trek series. He was in an episode of the original series in 1968, and then one episode each of *Deep Space Nine* and *Voyager* in 1996. When he died in July 2013, he was 91.

Charles Henry Simpson was born in 1913. Using the nickname Mickey, he entered films in 1939. Hollywood lore has it that John Ford gave him a bit in *Stagecoach*. The actor was with Ford in other films, including as Sam Clanton in 1946's *My Darling Clementine*. He was also a Clanton gang member, Frank McLowery, in 1957's *Gunfight at the O.K. Corral*.

Along with his role as henchman Powder in *The Lone Ranger*, Simpson worked under producer Willis Goldbeck's direction in *Ten Tall Men* in 1951. Between 1950 and 1956, he was in 13 *Lone Ranger* TV episodes. Only actor Lane Bradford guest starred more often. Mickey's first was #59, "Drink of Water," and his last was #192, "The Letter Bride."

His big hulking frame made him a most formidable foe. In the early 1950s, he was on ten episodes of *The Range Rider*. Between 1956 and 1962, he appeared on nine *Cheyenne* shows, where he was a perfect antagonist for big Clint Walker. Heart failure took the life of 71-year-old Mickey Simpson in 1985.

Henchman Goss in *The Lone Ranger* was played by Zon Murray. Born in 1910 with the first name Emery (Zon was his middle name), he became prolific during the 1940s as henchmen in various "B" Westerns. He was also in Kirk Douglas' first Western, 1951's *Along the Great Divide*.

With a mustache and sneering good looks, Murray was seen in many Western TV series of the 1950s and 1960s. Between 1950 and 1955, the actor appeared in a dozen *Cisco Kid* shows. And he was in a half dozen each of both *The Lone Ranger* (1953–57) and *The Life and Legend of Wyatt Earp* (1955–61).

Murray's initial *Ranger* episode was with John Hart's masked man, #97's "Trader Boggs." His last episode was the series' next to last, #220's "Blind Witness." The actor's final role was in the 1965 Western *Requiem for a Gunfighter*. He died in 1979 when he was 68.

"The stuntmen are frequently in action, belting each other, leaping off cliffs, tumbling down the sides of mountains and fully earning every cent they make," said Bosley Crowther in his February 1956 *New York Times* review of *The Lone Ranger*. Certainly those words apply to the film's best action sequence, where the Masked Man jumps from Silver onto his enemy Cassidy and both men then fall uncontrollably down the steep hillside. Bill Ward doubled for Clayton Moore here and Bob Morgan for Robert Wilke. It proved so dangerous that Moore thought they might be killed.

Robert Drew Morgan (1916–99) began doing stunts on 1947's *Dark Passage*, a Humphrey Bogart drama. With over 60 credits as a stunt-man, Morgan's skills were used in at least six Randolph Scott Westerns in the early 1950s. *The Big Country* (1958), *The Alamo, Spartacus* (1960) and *How the West Was Won* (1962) were Bob Morgan's biggest films stunt-wise. While making the latter epic, he lost one leg while shooting the climactic train sequence.

Bill Ward was born in 1926. He doubled for Clayton Moore in both *The Lone Ranger* and in 1952's *Buffalo Bill in Tomahawk Territory*. Seven *Lone Ranger* TV episodes featured Ward as an actor. All were in the first two seasons.

A good bit of the feature's exterior shooting was done in breath-taking Kanab, Utah. This included the big fight using Ward and Morgan. The fifth TV season of new episodes in color also used this location, as well as equally stunning locations in Lone Pine and Sonora, California.

During filming of the feature, there was a flash flood in Kanab. It swept through the canyon setting and carried away movie cameras and generators. Jay Silverheels and Clayton Moore were among those who had to scramble to safety.

The Kanab Movie Ranch, five miles north of town, was located in Kanab Canyon or, as it was also known, Angel Canyon. Other TV series which used the site included *Have Gun, Will Travel* and *Gunsmoke*. Feature films also included 1969's *Mackenna's Gold* and 1976's *The Outlaw Josey Wales*.

My favorite part of *The Lone Ranger* was filmed in Bronson Canyon. The location was actually part of Los Angeles' Griffith Park. This is when our masked hero is rescued by Silver after being shot and falling down a hillside. The Ranger is too weakened to get up but has the strength to hold onto Silver's stirrup as the horse drags him to water. Even now seeing him hurt and vulnerable, and with David Buttolph's music score making it especially touching, I get misty-eyed.

For this sequence, Silver #1—or as Clayton again called him, "good old Liver Lip"—was brought in to pull the actor along the ground. It was felt that Silver. #2, the steed predominately used at the time, might kick out and possibly cause an injury.

Filming also took place at Warner Brothers in Burbank, California, where a good many Western television shows were shot. Included in this roster were *Cheyenne, Sugarfoot, Bronco and Maverick*.

That same *New York Times* review of *The Lone Ranger* observed, "[I]t is still the same old script—or a patchwork of pieces out of others." A February 1956 reviewer for *America* magazine felt that the movie's appeal "would appear to be limited strictly to small boys of all ages."

The film proved that fans of the TV series would pay to see their beloved heroes, the Lone Ranger and Tonto, on the big screen. Its box office earnings ($1,550,000) were big enough to warrant a sequel. *The Lone Ranger* placed #65 on the list of 1956's big moneymakers.

I would not agree with Phil Hardy (*The Encyclopedia of Western Movies*) that Clayton Moore's portrayal was "wooden"; in my view, Moore was never more exciting and charismatic. Yet I would agree with that same author's assessment of the film as "a masterpiece of children's cinema." While there are assuredly elements of other Westerns in this one—white men disguised as Indians, a child's endangerment, cavalry to the rescue and so on—the same holds true for the very greatest of Westerns.

Seven

The 1958 Film
The Lone Ranger
and the Lost City of Gold

Here he comes! Thundering up the West's deadliest trail....
Blasting his way into the fabled city of gold!
—tagline for the film

A Jack Wrather Production. Released by United Artists in June 1958.
80 minutes. Eastmancolor.

Credits:
Producer: Sherman A. Harris.
Director: Lesley Selander.
Screenplay: Robert Schaefer, Eric Freiwald.
Photography: Kenneth Peach.
Editor: Robert S. Golden.
Art Director: James D. Vance.
Set Decorator: Charles Thompson.
Makeup: Layne Britton.
Music: Les Baxter.

Cast:
Clayton Moore (The Lone Ranger); Jay Silverheels (Tonto); Douglas
Kennedy (Ross Brady); Charles Watts (Sheriff Oscar Matthison);
Noreen Nash (Frances Henderson); Lisa Montell (Paviva); Ralph
Moody (Padre Vincente Esteban); Norman Fredric (Dr. James Rolfe);
John Miljan (Tomache); Maurice Jara (Redbird); Bill Henry (Travers);
Lane Bradford (Wilson); Belle Mitchell (Caulama); Bob Woodward
(Henchman).

Synopsis: The Lone Ranger and Tonto chase after six hooded
raiders who have attacked a wagon and killed an Indian. When the
Ranger catches up to one of the men, a fight breaks out and the raider

plummets to his death off a cliff. An infant boy belonging to the slain Indian is found safe by Silver, the Ranger's stallion. The child is taken by Tonto and the Ranger to their friend Padre Vincente Esteban's mission, where Indian maiden Paviva is captivated by the baby.

Tonto goes to the nearby town of San Doria to fetch a doctor, James Rolfe, for the baby. While in town, Tonto is waylaid just because he is an Indian by Sheriff Oscar Matthison and some toughs. Dr. Rolfe comes to Tonto's aid.

The Ranger and Tonto are told about an Indian ceremony by an Indian brave named Redbird. Many years earlier, a ball of fire (the Ranger discerns that it was a meteorite) destroyed Spanish soldiers endangering Redbird's ancestors.

At the ranch of widow Frances Henderson, hooded raider leader Ross Brady gives her a medallion piece taken from the baby's dead father. Placing it next to another piece, Frances and Brady vainly attempt to decipher its message. Three more medallion pieces are needed to reveal the location of Cibola, one of the seven fabled cities of gold.

Masquerading as bounty hunter Bret Reagan, the Lone Ranger visits Frances with the intent of learning about her involvement. A jealous Brady interrupts them, later warning Frances that she is his woman.

Back at the mission, Paviva's love for Dr. Rolfe is apparent. She is frustrated by his refusal to admit he too is an Indian. Rolfe feels that only by keeping it a secret can he make enough money to build a hospital for his people.

Two more medallion pieces are stolen and an Indian killed. The Masked Man and Tonto learn from Chief Tomache that five Indians each held a medallion piece, including a now unknown grandson. After the Lone Ranger captures a raider, Travers, Redbird takes him from jail and tries to force him to inform on his cohorts in crime. Brady shoots him down from afar, but Travers still implicates his boss.

Again posing as the bounty hunter, the Ranger is able to get Frances to reveal her involvement by pretending to have the fifth medallion piece. He then rides off to send a telegram to alert a marshal. When the bigoted sheriff injures Tonto, Rolfe admits his Indian heritage. As Tomache's grandson, he has the last medallion piece.

Rolfe and Paviva then go with the baby to Tomache's village. Battling the raiders, Tonto kills one and Rolfe another. Arriving to help, the Ranger is forced to kill raider Wilson. Silver helps by stopping Brady from abducting the baby. The Ranger wounds Brady, who escapes with Rolfe's medallion piece.

When Brady returns to Frances' ranch, she is only concerned with the whole medallion. Slapping her and taking all the pieces, Brady is

Jay Silverheels and Clayton Moore size up a situation in this scene from *The Lone Ranger and the Lost City of Gold* (1958).

killed by Frances with an axe. The Ranger rides up and apprehends her.

The message on the medallion takes the Ranger, Tonto, Paviva, Rolfe and the padre to a cave. Inside they find gold stalactites and stalagmites everywhere amidst the hidden city of Cibola. Paviva seems especially enthralled knowing James will now have his hospital, and together as husband and wife they will raise the baby.

The *Lone Ranger* TV series had ended its run when Clayton Moore and Jay Silverheels were notified about another feature film. Moore was on tour as the Ranger in Reading, Pennsylvania, when he received the news. "I was delighted," he said. "I knew that the first feature, *The Lone Ranger*, had been a big hit, and I hoped we would get to make another." He and Jay liked the script for *The Lone Ranger and the Lost City of Gold*, written by Robert Schaefer and Eric Freiwald. Prior to the feature, the writing team of Schaefer and Freiwald worked together on 13 *Lone Ranger* TV episodes. Among their other writing collaborations were a dozen episodes of *The Gene Autry Show* between 1952 and 1954, and 32 TV episodes of Autry's *Annie Oakley* series from 1954 to 1957. They also collaborated on 120 episodes of Jack Wrather's *Lassie* series between 1959 and 1973. Freiwald later worked as a writer on the soap opera *The Young and the Restless*. Freiwald was 82 when he died in January 2010. Schaefer, who died in December 2006, was 80.

Instead of Warner Brothers, United Artists released this "All New! All-Out Adventure!" for Wrather's production outfit. Sherman A. Harris produced and Lesley Selander directed. *The Encyclopedia of Western Movies* called it a "lackluster sequel."

Sherman Allison Harris (1909–80) produced the last season of *Lone Ranger* TV shows. Between 1958 and 1960, he was executive producer on 74 episodes of *Lassie*. Prior to these shows, Harris produced 19 episodes of a 1950–51 dramatic anthology series called *Stars Over Hollywood*. His initial work on a TV series with a Western theme was as production manager on *Cowboy G-Men*.

Harris started out in motion pictures as a production manager during the 1940s. The first film was *Cheers for Miss Bishop*, a 1941 drama about a woman devoting her life to teaching. *The Lone Ranger and the Lost City of Gold* was his last motion picture.

Born in 1900, Lesley Selander was perhaps the most proficient director of "B" Western films during the 1930s and 1940s. His first was *Ride 'Em Cowboy* (1936) with Buck Jones. Other popular Western stars directed by Selander included Tim Holt, Sunset Carson and Bill Elliott.

Selander made more than 25 Hopalong Cassidy films with William Boyd. The initial one was *Hopalong Rides Again* in 1937, and the last was *Forty Thieves* in 1944. In 1956, two years before his *Lone Ranger* adventure, he directed the Randolph Scott Western *Tall Man Riding*.

Selander's first TV directing jobs were a couple of episodes of *Cowboy G-Men* in 1952. For Jack Wrather, he also helmed 54 episodes of *Lassie* between 1955 and 1959. When he passed away in 1979, Selander was 79.

"Typical Lone Ranger Western is fine for younger audiences," said Leonard Maltin in his *Classic Movie Guide* book. This was especially true of the enchanting friendship between those wonderful storybook-like characters played by Moore and Silverheels. Yet when first seeing the film as a boy, I was more than a little stunned by the violence in the climactic scene where Noreen Nash's Frances Henderson throws an axe right into the back of Douglas Kennedy's Ross Brady.

Always a delight when donning disguises, Clayton was given yet another one to extend his range as an actor. Yet his Bret Reagan is not the usual tough bounty hunter in dirty Western garb and carrying a gun as seen in films and on television. Here he is a real Southern gentleman and smooth talker.

Moore's Masked Man gets into some dandy fistfights and gunplay during the course of the story, and it's always nice to see Silverheels in on the action too. One especially captivating sequence has Jay's Tonto coming to the defense of Lisa Montell's proud young Indian woman against Charles Watts' racist sheriff.

The heroes' horses, Silver and Scout, have some nice moments. Looking after the baby's well-being, Silver is brave and amusing both. When Tonto awakens one morning, he shares a cute scene with Scout lying beside him and hogging the blanket.

Riding off on their faithful steeds at the end of the 1956 and 1958 films, Tonto and the Lone Ranger are praised by men of the cloth.

Edward Colmans' padre in the first and Ralph Moody as Padre Esteban in the second each give a moving farewell to our heroes.

Ralph Roy Moody was born in 1886. His first work as an actor in Westerns was on radio with *The Roy Rogers Show* in the 1940s. One of his early Western film roles was in the 1950 classic *The Gunfighter*. Moody was especially prolific doing series TV during the 1950s and 1960s. His initial TV appearances were as Indian chiefs on three *Lone Ranger* episodes between 1949 and 1950. He was approaching the age of 63 when he did the first one, "The Renegades." Between 1952 and 1959, Moody appeared in various roles on the popular dramatic series *Dragnet*. Western fans may remember him best as Doc Burrage on nine episodes of *The Rifleman* between 1961 and 1963. At age 84, the character actor died from a heart attack in 1971.

Growing up watching TV Westerns, I had quite a crush on Lisa Montell. She was one of the most beautifully stunning actresses of her day. And she was also quite spirited as proven by her role as Paviva in *The Lone Ranger and the Lost City of Gold*. When she was born in 1933, her name was Irena Ludmilla Viadimirovna Augustinovich. Her dark hair and sultry beauty made her perfect for playing ethnic roles. A 1955 *Gene Autry* episode was her initial work on a Western. Among others she appeared in were two episodes of *Cheyenne* and two of *Sugarfoot*. The actress also did film work including *Daughter of the Sun God*, which seemed a most fitting title for her. Made in 1953, it was not released until 1962; and she then left show business to devote her life to the Baha'i Faith. As Lisa Janti (she was once wed to actor David Janti), she wrote a book on her religion, *Baha'i: The New Vision*.

Paviva's love interest in the *Lone Ranger* film, Dr. James Rolfe, was played with both humility and fortitude by Norman Fredric. He was born in 1924 (real name: Frederick Joseph Foote) and began working in films and TV in the 1950s; he played Kaseem, manservant of Jungle Jim, in the 1955–56 *Jungle Jim* TV series. Between 1958 and 1965, when his acting career ended, he was known as Dean Fredericks. Using that name, he starred in the 1958–59 TV series *Steve Canyon*, based on the popular comic strip. He even had his dark hair dyed blonde to match the heroic flying ace. In 1961, the actor was the astronaut hero of *The Phantom Planet*. Fredericks played Indians in the Disney film *Savage Sam* (1963) and in the Daniel Boone mini-series on the *Wonderful*

World of Color TV show in 1960 and 1961. He was 75 when he passed away in June 1999.

Also seen in *Lost City of Gold* are John Miljan as Chief Tomache and Maurice Jara as Redbird. Like Frank deKova's Chief Red Hawk in the 1956 *Lone Ranger* movie, Miljan's Chief Tomache was an ancient figure with the wisdom of all the ages. Jovan Miljanovic was born in 1892 and as John Miljan he entered silent films in 1924. For his sound debut, he introduced the 1927 promotional trailer for the first talking motion picture, *The Jazz Singer*. Over the years he would prove his worth in both heroic and villainous roles. For director Cecil B. DeMille, the actor played several roles, including General George A. Custer in 1936's The *Plainsman* and the old blind man in the mud pit in 1956's *The Ten Commandments*.

Clayton Moore's Ranger and Jay Silverheels' Tonto are moved by their encounter with John Miljan's wise chief in *The Lone Ranger and the Lost City of Gold*.

Included in Miljan's TV credits were an episode of *The Adventures of Jim Bowie* in 1957 and a *Broken Arrow* in 1958. The 1958 *Lone Ranger* tale proved to be his last film appearance. He died at age 67 in 1960.

One of Maurice Jara's early roles was in 1951's *Pals of the Golden West*, last in the Roy Rogers film series. Jara also made his first TV appearance in 1951 on an episode of *Sky King*. As Saul R. Jara, he was born in 1922. In addition to portraying Redbird in the 1958 film, Jara played Indians on three episodes of the *Lone Ranger* TV series between 1952 and 1957. The initial one, "The Condemned Man," was with John Hart's Ranger, the other two, "Enfield Rifle" and "The Courage of Tonto," were with Moore. Jara was also seen on three episodes of *Death Valley Days*. Perhaps his most prominent film role was in the 1956 contemporary Western *Giant*. Jara passed away in 1995 at age 72.

The Lone Ranger and the Lost City of Gold has a villain and villainess who can more than hold their own with the best that Hollywood

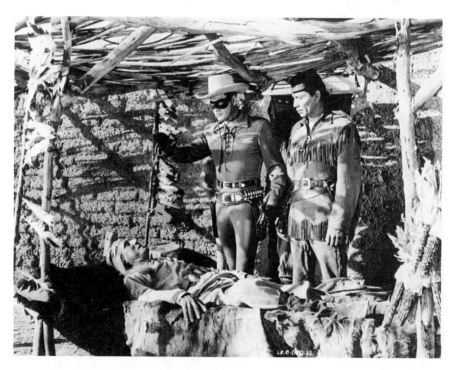

Clayton Moore and Jay Silverheels confront Maurice Jara in *The Lone Ranger and the Lost City of Gold.*

conjured up. With over 200 film and TV credits, Douglas Kennedy always seemed a force to be reckoned with. Most assuredly it was due to his formidable presence, which was put to good use as Ross Brady. As Douglas Richards Kennedy, he was born in 1915. His impressive lists of TV Westerns included his own series in the 1955–56 season, *Steve Donovan, Western Marshal*. He was certainly adept at playing both good guys and bad guys. In various roles he was also seen on six episodes of the *Lone Ranger* series between 1950 and 1955; the first was "A Pardon for Curley" and the last was "Trigger Finger." As Sheriff Fred Madden, the actor was seen on 20 episodes of the series *The Big Valley* between 1967 and 1969. Other recurring roles were on three episodes of *Zorro* in 1959 and two on *The Life and Legend of Wyatt Earp* that same year. He was only 57 when he died in August 1973.

While Kennedy's Brady may be the leader of the hooded raiders, he has his hands full trying to wrest control of their dirty operations from Frances Henderson's tigress. Noreen Nash's charm and beauty never mask her cold, calculating heart but make her appear even more alluring.

As Noreen Roth, she was born in 1924. Her last name was changed following a film role in the 1945 drama The *Southerner*. Her first Western film appearance was in 1947's *The Red Stallion*.

A 1952 *Hopalong Cassidy* episode was her initial foray into TV Westerns. The actress also appeared in a 1953 *Lone Ranger* episode with John Hart, "A Stage for Mademoiselle." On the 1956 series The *Charlie Farrell Show*, she was a regular as Doris Mayfield. Nash's last Western TV work was as Agatha Colton on two episodes of *Yancy Derringer*. At one time she was married to actor James Whitmore.

In "Lady Killer," an episode of the *Lone Ranger* TV series, Nan Leslie played a role similar to Miss Nash's in the 1958 film: Lela Anson, a schemer involved in killings and robberies.

In *Lost City of Gold*, all the top bad guys meet violent fates, especially Lane Bradford's Wilson. While gunning for Tonto, he has a knife thrown into his chest. Surprisingly still able to walk away, he tries to ambush the Ranger and is then shot down.

Bradford had an even more impressive list of TV series credits than Douglas Kennedy. For Jack Wrather, he worked on three *Sergeant Preston of the Yukon* episodes and five *Lassie*s. His full name at birth in 1922 was John Myrtland LeVarre, Jr.; he and Kennedy died just over two months apart in 1973.

William Albert Henry was born in 1914. His film debut was as a child actor in the 1925 silent *Lord Jim*. In 1936's *Tarzan Escapes*, he played the cousin of Maureen O'Sullivan's Jane. He was often billed just as Bill Henry; his first TV Western series work was on *The Gene Autry Show* in 1950. He became a regular player in John Ford films, including Ford's last two Westerns *The Man Who Shot Liberty Valance* (1962) and *Cheyenne Autumn* (1964). I especially remember Henry as Dr. Sutherland from John Wayne's *The Alamo* (1960).

Along with henchman Travers in *Lost City of Gold*, the actor appeared in three episodes of the TV series in its final season, "Quicksand," "The Twisted Track" and "Christmas Story." When he died in 1982, Bill Henry was 67 years old.

Charles Watts' Sheriff Matthison is not a criminal, yet he is an oafish bore. Above all, the character is a danger to the Indians because of his prejudice. The other townsfolk finally have enough of him and turn away from him. Born in 1912, Watts was a schoolteacher before turning to acting in 1950. Portly and gabby, he was well-regarded for his work on both film and TV. He did three episodes of *The Lone Ranger*, "The Star Witness" in the first season and "Thieves' Money" and "Paid in Full" in the second. Often Watts' mannerisms bordered on the inane or comedic even in the *Ranger* film. This was particularly the case for his sitcom work in assorted roles during the late 1950s and early 1960s on such shows as *The Many Loves of Dobie Gillis* and *Dennis the Menace*. Watts died of cancer when he was only 54 in 1966.

Indian prejudice was reflected in both the 1956 and 1958 *Lone Ranger* motion pictures. Various episodes of the TV series addressed the issue as well. This was commendable especially for films and shows regarded as children's programming. The TV episodes "Backtrail" and "Counterfeit Redskins" dealt with Indians accused of crimes perpetrated by white men. In the appropriately titled "Framed for Murder," Tonto faces an unjust murder charge. At the same time, all Indians were not law-abiding. In "Message to Fort Apache," Indians illegally buy guns; and in a similar episode, "Enfield Rifle," renegade Indians get hold of a smuggled repeating rifle.

Yet the majority of stories were about Tonto and the Lone Ranger fighting outlawry in all forms in the Old West. This was most vivid in the initial three TV episodes and both follow-up films as well. Others joining our heroes in the fight were lawmen. Lane Chandler, one of the Texas Rangers from the 1938 serial, played an aging sheriff in the TV episode "Masked Deputy."

Good and bad lawmen provided storylines for the series and the films. John Pickard's sheriff in the first film rises above his own issues to become a U.S. marshal; but not Charles Watts' lawman in the second, who should be ashamed to wear the badge. One TV episode, "The Sheriff's Son," focused on an outlaw sent to jail by his own father, a lawman.

Parents and their offspring were part of the plots of the 1956 film and episodes of the series. In "A Son by Adoption," a boy discovers that his real father is an outlaw. Tris Coffin, the first episode's Texas Ranger captain, was a father whose son sees him gunned down and then becomes sheriff in "The Avenger."

In my favorite shows, the Lone Ranger is in defense of his honor. Two examples come to mind. In "The Masked Rider," the Ranger must find a killer posing as him; and in "Gold Train," he is blamed for crimes committed by a masked outlaw called the Dude.

Enhancing the Lone Ranger's TV adventures were often brilliant and bizarre landscapes; and perhaps not put to better use than in *The Lone Ranger and the Lost City of Gold*. Locations in and around Tucson, Arizona, were utilized. Just south of town, the Old Tucson film studios were second only to those in Hollywood for the production of Western TV shows and movies in the 1950s. Two of my favorites were shot there, *Gunfight at the O.K. Corral* and *Rio Bravo*. Both *Lost City of Gold* and the earlier TV series used the site. For the film, the San Xavier de Bac Mission and the San Xavier Tohono O'odham Reservation in Tucson were also used. Forty miles from town were the Sierrita Mountains seen in the motion picture.

The most impressive location was that part of the Sonoran Desert in Arizona southwest of Tucson. Spectacular and even surreal were its massive cactus called the organ pipe and saguaro. Only in the Sonoran does the saguaro cactus apparently grow wild and free.

If only for its stunning scenery alone, this Lone Ranger tale rises above any shortcomings. While the film was a box office hit, it was not considered as successful or exciting as the first one. Yet their second one did have the distinction of being part of the 25th anniversary of the Lone Ranger legacy, first started on radio in 1933.

The 1958 feature also boasted a song, "Hi Yo Silver," written by Les Baxter and Lenny Adelson. First heard at the beginning, it tells the tale of the hero's origin during the ambush with his fellow Texas Rangers. When the song was released as a 45 RPM single, it was a big hit. It's now a collector's item.

That brief retelling of the Lone Ranger's origin in the film, including the song, were used to introduce a repackaging by Jack Wrather of the final season's 39 TV episodes. They were then turned into 13 features for syndication to television. Each feature was 77 minutes long and ran under the banner title *The Adventures of the Lone Ranger*. Then in turn each one, presenting three episodes, had its own separate title:

1. *Champions of Justice* incorporated "Blind Witness," "Clover in the Dust" and "The Angel and the Outlaw."
2. *Count the Clues*: "Wooden Rifle," "The Sheriff of Smoke Tree" and "Ghost Town Fury."
3. *Justice of the West*: "Outlaw Masquerade," "Quicksand" and "No Handicap."
4. *The Lawless*: "Slim's Boy," "The Return of Don Pedro O'Sullivan" and "The Tarnished Star."
5. *Masquerade*: "The Turning Point," "Code of Honor" and "Dead Eye."
6. *More than Magic*: "Outlaws in Greasepaint," "White Hawk's Decision" and "Hot Spell in Panamint."
7. *Not Above-Suspicion*: "The Avenger, " "Mission for Tonto" and "Journey to San Carlos."
8. *One Mask Too Many*: "The Prince of Buffalo Gap," "Canuck" and "Counterfeit Mask."
9. *The Scorch*: "Christmas Story," "The Cross of Santa Domingo" and "The Breaking Point."
10. *Tale of Gold*: "Quarterhorse War," "A Harp for Hannah" and "Decision for Chris McKeever."
11. *The Trackers*: "The Twisted Track," "Trouble at Tylerville" and "Ghost Canyon."

12. *The Truth*: "The Banker's Son," "The Letter Bride" and "The Law and Miss Aggie."

13. *Vengeance Vow*: "Two Against Two," "A Message from Abe" and "The Courage of Tonto."

Both the 1956 *Lone Ranger* movie and *Lost City of Gold* are available on home video. The DVD *The Lone Ranger Double Feature* includes the two together. A few of the *Adventures of the Lone Ranger* features, including *Justice of the West* and *The Trackers*, were available on VHS.

Eight

The Animated Cartoons

In this forge upon this anvil was hammered out a man
who became a legend ... a daring and resourceful man
who hated thievery and oppression.
—from the opening narration of *The Lone Ranger*
animated TV series (1966–69)

Before the Lone Ranger came to life in animated form, he was seen in newspaper comic strips beginning in September 1938. They were distributed by King Features Syndicate until December 1971. Fran Striker contributed his writing skills to the comic strip before others took over. In 1939, initial artist Ed Kressy was replaced by Charles Flanders, who then drew the strip to its end.

The New York Times Syndicate ran a new Lone Ranger comic strip from 1981 to 1984. Russ Heath was the artist and Cary Bates the writer. There have also been many comic books published over the years. Western Publishing and its partner Dell Comics began the first comic book series in 1948. Dell even published a comic book adaptation of the 1956 film.

In 1962, Dell ended its association with both the *Lone Ranger* comic books and Western Publishing; and the latter then started the Gold Key comic books. While Gold Key Comics started out simply reprinting the Dell material, new stories were printed from 1975 until 1977.

Other comic book publishers included Topps with four *Lone Ranger and Tonto* issues, as well as Dynamite Entertainment beginning in 2006. The latter changed Captain Reid's first name to James; and he was the father of both John and Dan.

The 1930s Lone Ranger Cartoon, as it was known, was regarded as the very first animated one. Running two minutes, 40 seconds. Producer Roy Meredith made it for a company called Pathegrams. The cartoon was scored with the William Tell Overture, with dialog in intertitles as in silent films. Tonto and the Lone Ranger protect a rancher against cattle rustlers. It is part of a 2001 video called *The Lone Ranger: The Lost Episodes*. It also can be seen on YouTube.

On January 7, 1939, Warner Brothers released a black-and-white cartoon parody of the Lone Ranger to theaters. Titled *The Lone Stranger and Porky*, it was part of the studio's Looney Tunes series of animated shorts. Leon Schlesinger and Raymond Katz produced this short, and the director was Robert Clampett. In it, Porky Pig is rescued from the Villain (and that is his name) by the Lone Stranger. Especially amusing was Silver, the Stranger's horse, falling in love with the bad guy's horse.

Another cartoon parody, MGM's *The Lonesome Stranger*, was released on November 23, 1940. Hugh Harman was the producer of this nine-minute Technicolor cartoon in which the Lonesome Stranger and Silver clash with the Killer Diller Boys, a trio of bad hombres. When a gunpowder blast sends the Stranger careening into the three, he loses his pants in the bargain.

In the 1960s, the Lone Ranger and Tonto began a series of adventures in animated form on television, as part of the Saturday morning lineup for kids. Jack Wrather's Lone Ranger Television and Format Films in Hollywood collaborated on the show. Format's producers were Herb Klynn and Jilles Engel.

CBS network aired the color, half-hour *Lone Ranger* animated series from September 10, 1966, to September 6, 1969. Three episodes per show were seen in a half-hour format and in color on 24 shows to November 18, 1967. The initial three episodes were "The Trickster," "The Crack of Doom" and "The Human Dynamo."

Two more original shows were aired on January 6 and January 13, 1968. The first one had a pair of episodes, "Lash and the Arrow" and "Spectre of Death"; and the last had a solo episode, "Mr. Midas."

The animation was created at the Halas and Batchelor cartoon studio in London, England. Especially effective was Walt Peregoy's background artwork, in which black penciled borders were used with torn or cut colored paper. The results proved striking and even innovative. Yet the animated styling for actual character presentation was considered fundamental at best.

Batman, the live action TV series which first aired in January 1966, undoubtedly influenced the *Lone Ranger* animated series with its fantastic story lines and villains. While the former had such performers and characters as Cesar Romero's Joker and Julie Newmar's Catwoman, the latter's guest voices included Hans Conried as Mephisto and Agnes Moorehead as Black Widow.

The Lone Ranger and Tonto were voiced by Michael Rye and Shepard Menken, respectively, and they seemed on a par with superheroes like Batman and Robin. In particular their marksmanship with pistol and bow made them appear superhuman.

John Michael Riorden Billsbury was born in 1918. As Michael Rye, he became proficient showcasing his voice talents on radio. His initial radio work was as the announcer on *The Cisco Kid* from 1943 to 1945. Between 1944 and 1946, he had the title role on radio's *Jack Armstrong, the All-American Boy.*

In addition to his stint as the Lone Ranger in the first animated series, Rye did the voice for the Green Lantern superhero in several of the Hanna-Barbera animated TV shows of the 1970s and 1980s. The initial Green Lantern role was on the *Super Friends* series in 1977.

Live-action TV shows also offered Rye acting roles, including one episode each of *The Adventures of Rin Tin Tin* and *Wagon Train.* Before he retired in the late 1990s, Michael Rye was doing commercials for radio and TV. At the age of 94, he died in 2012.

Tonto on the animated series was played by Shepard Menken. Born in 1921, he was still a youngster when he started out on radio with children's programming. He was credited with appearances in 17 motion pictures, including the 1951 Biblical epic *David and Bathsheba.* Also in 1951, Menken appeared in assorted roles on a few episodes of the popular *I Love Lucy* TV series. He was also seen on two popular Western shows in 1965, *The Wild Wild West* and *The Big Valley.*

Menken was most widely known for his voice work on animated TV shows and commercials. The shows included *The Alvin Show* in 1961 and *Spider-Man and His Amazing Friends* in 1981. He did voices for commercials including Mattel Toys and StarKist Tuna. In 1999, he died at age 77.

The Wild Wild West was clearly another influence on the *Lone Ranger* animated program with its science fiction themes. Included were death rays, robots and colorful villains. Another villain, Tiny Tom (voiced by Dick Beals) bore more than a passing resemblance to Michael Dunn's Dr. Loveless from *Wild Wild West.*

While youngsters of the day ate it all up, viewers of the original live action *Lone Ranger* series, like myself, were a bit perplexed by the changes for our heroes. Nonetheless it was still entertaining. Helping things along were the compelling music arrangements by Vic Schoen and composer Johnny Gregory's work, with an especially forceful presentation of Rossini's *William Tell Overture*. During the 1980s, it was this treatment of the famed theme music which was used for the TV syndication ads of the live action series.

The Lone Ranger (1966–69)

Art and Animation Credits:
Story Director: Tom Dagenais
Story Sketches: Lynn Goller, Sherman Labby, Gary Lund, Walt Peregoy
Ink and Paint Artists: Amaya Ash, Zora Bubica, Wendy Hawthorn
Background Artists: Tom Bailey, Thelma G. Dufton, David Elvin, Zoran Janjic, Vern Jorgensen, Ted Lewis, Gary Lund, Carlos Marietto, Bob McIntosh, Chris Miles, Walt Peregoy, Gil Potter
Animators: Ruben Apodaca, Bob Bransford, Geoff Collins, Ed Friedman, Peter Gardiner, Alan Green, Terence Harrison, Dave Livesey, Amby Paliwoda, Yvonne Pearsall, Virgil Ross, Laurie Sharpe, Clive A. Smith, Hank Smith, David Whittam, Stan Wilkins.

ANIMATED SERIES EPISODES AND AIRDATES
OF *THE LONE RANGER*

First Season

1. "The Trickster," "The Cracks of Doom," "The Human Dynamo" (9/10/66)
2. "Ghost Riders," "Wrath of the Sun God," "Day of The Dragon" (9/17/66)
3. "The Secret Army of General X," "The Cat People," "Night of the Vampire" (9/24/66)
4. "Bear Claw," "The Hunter and the Hunted," "Mephisto" (10/1/66)
5. "Revenge of the Mole," "Frog People," "Terror in Toyland" (10/8/66)
6. "Black Mask of Revenge," "The Sacrifice," "Puppetmaster" (10/15/66)

7. "Valley of the Dead," "Forest of Death," "The Fly" (10/22/66)
8. "A Time to Die," "Ghost Tribe of Comanche Flat," "Attack of the Lilliputians" (10/29/66)
9. "Circus of Death," "The Brave," "Cult of the Black Widow" (11/5/60)
10. "El Conquistador," "Show Creature," "The Prairie Pirate" (11/12/66)
11. "Man of Silver," "Nightmare in Whispering Pine," "Sabotage" (11/19/66)
12. "Mastermind," "The Lost Tribe of Golden Giants," "Monster of Scavenger Crossing" (1/7/67)
13. "The Black Panther," "Thomas the Great," "Island of the Black Widow" (1/14/67)

Second Season

14. "Paddle Wheeling Pirates," "A Day at Death's Head Pass," "The Mad, Mad, Mad, Mad Scientist" (9/9/67)
15. "The Kid," "Stone Hawk," "Sky Raiders" (9/16/67)
16. "The Man from Pinkerton," "Tonto and the Devil Spirit," "The Deadly Glassman" (9/23/67)
17. "Black Knight," "Taka," "Fire Rain" (9/30/67)
18. "The Secret of Warlock," "Wolfmaster," "Death Hunt" (10/7/67)
19. "Terrible Tiny Tom," "Fire Monster," "The Iron Giant" (10/14/67)
20. "Town Tamers Inc.," "Curse of the Devil Doll," "It Came from Below" (10/21/67)
21. "Black Arrow," "The Rainmaker," "Flight of the Hawk" (10/28/67)
22. "The Avenger," "Battle at Barnaby's Bend," "Puppetmaster's Revenge" (11/4/67)
23. "Reign of the Queen Bee," "Wingdom of Terror," "Quicksilver" (11/11/67)
24. "The Legend of Cherokee Smith," "The Day the West Stood Still," "Border Rats" (11/18/67)

25. "Lash and the Arrow," "The Spectre of Death" (1/6/68)
26. "Mr. Midas" (1/13/68)

The show aired on Saturday mornings from 11:30 to 12 in its initial season; 1:00–1:30 p.m. its second; and 1:30–2:00 p.m. in the third. The last season was also entirely made up of reruns.

On September 13, 1980, *The New Adventures of the Lone Ranger* combined with previous episodes of the *Tarzan, Lord of the Jungle* animated series first seen in 1976. Thus was created another animated show, *Tarzan/Lone Ranger Adventure Hour*, for Saturday daytime viewing on CBS-TV.

For these *Lone Ranger* adventures, Filmation Associates in Reseda, California, was responsible for the animation. When the series was still in preparation, Filmation wanted Clayton Moore and Jay Silverheels to lend their voice talents for their most celebrated roles.

But Jay passed away on March 5, 1980, at the age of 62. He had suffered a stroke earlier in 1974, and his health was poor thereafter. At his memorial service, Clayton spoke about their genuine friendship. After Jay's body was cremated, his ashes were taken to Canada's Six Nations Reservation where he was born.

While one of Filmation's producers, Lou Scheimer, tried to persuade Clayton to do the role, the actor felt he needed a certain amount of rehearsal time. The producer failed to convince him that he needed only to read lines from a script in his hand.

William Conrad did the voice of the Lone Ranger. On-screen he was billed as J. Darnoc (Darnoc is Conrad spelled backwards). The performer may not have wanted it known that he was involved at this stage in his career on a cartoon series; or it could have just been his sense of humor in play. Conrad was then between his two popular TV series dramas *Cannon* (1971–76) and *Jake and the Fatman* (1987–92). Conrad's distinctive, deep voice was certainly a giveaway as the Masked Man. Years earlier, he played the role of Matt Dillon on the radio series *Gunsmoke*.

Born John William Cann (1920–94), Conrad was an actor, director and even producer. Among his many directorial credits for TV were two episodes of the James Arness version of *Gunsmoke*. At the beginning of his film career, he was known for his menacing roles; a standout was as one of the hired guns in 1946's *The Killers*.

Tonto on the new animated *Lone Ranger* was voiced by actor Ivan Naranjo. Especially noticeable was the character's extensive and concise use of the English language. It was surely a reflection of the 1980s rather than an extension of any of the earlier broken English spoken by the various Tontos in both film and TV. Naranjo, who was born in 1937, actually had Native American roots. He was able to claim ancestry in both the Southern Ute and Blackfeet Nations. His role as Tonto was apparently his only animated one. His live-action TV roles included comedy, drama and Western programs.

Naranjo portrayed Indian roles even in the non–Westerns. But as One Wolf, he was seen on six episodes in 1976 of the Jim Arness Western miniseries, *How the West Was Won*. He passed away in 2013 at age 76.

Filmation's animation was bigger and better than that offered from Format Productions (which that outfit was called with its earlier *Lone Ranger* series). An on-line review called the backgrounds "fantastic" and "almost 3-D in places."

Vern Jorgensen a background artist on the earlier series, again filled that position for Filmation. Ed Friedman, an animator on the initial *Lone Ranger*, was an animation director on the new series. Friedman was also a director on Filmation's *Tarzan, Lord of the Jungle*. In the 1977–78 TV season, it became the *Batman/Tarzan Adventure Hour*; the voices of Adam West and Burt Ward, the original live action TV series heroes, were heard as Batman and Robin.

For Filmation's two programs including the Lone Ranger, the series music was credited to Yvette Blais and Jeff Michael. The names were really aliases far Ray Ellis and Norm Prescott, respectively. Once more the *William Tell Overture* was used to good effect. Prescott was also one of the producers. The others were Don Christensen and the aforementioned Lou Scheimer.

The Tarzan/Lone Ranger Adventure Hour (1980–81) and *The Tarzan/Lone Ranger/Zorro Adventure Hour* (1981–82)

Art and Animation Credits:
Storyboard Director: Karl Geurs.
Storyboard Supervisors: Lonnie Lloyd, William Meugniot.

Storyboard Artists: Richard Hoberg, Larry Houston, Sean Joyce, Don Manuel, Paul Smith, Terry Windell.

Layout Supervisors: Herb Hazelton, Carol Lundberg.

Layout Artists: Rex Barron, Todd Falk, Kevin Frank, Sergio Garcia, Steve Gordon, Edward Haney, Clarence Hartman, Russell Heath, David Hoover, Richard Hoover, Mary Jorgensen, Mel Keefer, John Koch, Jim McLean, Skip Morgan, Phillip Norwood, Jesse Santos, Barton Seitz, David Stevens.

Background Artists: Barbara Benedetto, Alan Bodner Sheila Rae Brown, Ellen Caster, Dianne Erenberg, Vern Jorgensen, Pat Keppier, Tom O'Loughlin, Curt Perkins, Don Schweikert, Don Watson.

Head Animation Director: Gwen Wetzler.

Animation Directors: John Armstrong, Kent Butterworth, Ed Friedman, Lou Kachivas, Marsh Lamore, Ernie Schmidt, Kay Wright, Lou Zuko.

Animators: Thomas Baron, Arland Barron, James Brummett, Patrick Clark, Richard Coleman, James Davis, Edward DeMattia, Jeffery Etter, Lillian Evans, Rick Farmilow, Miguel Garcia, Michael Gerard, Lee Halpern, Karen Haus, Kennetha Hildebrand, Brett Hisey, Walt Kubiak, Stephen Marsh, Larry Miller, Gale Morgan, Frank Edward Olivares, Jack Ozark, William Pratt, William Recinos, Chrystal Russell, Sonja Ruta, Don Schloat, Cheryl Selleck, Larry Silverman, James Simon, Ka Woon Song, Michael Toth, Robert Tyler, Dardo Velez, Lawrence White.

ANIMATED SERIES EPISODES AND AIRDATES OF *THE TARZAN/LONE RANGER ADVENTURE HOUR*

First Season

1. "Hanga, the Night Monster" (9/13/80)
2. "The Yellowstone Conspiracy" (9/20/80)
3. "The Escape"(9/27/80)
4. "The Great Balloon Race" (10/4/80)
5. "The President Plot" (10/18/80)
6. "Tall Timber" (10/25/80)
7. "Blowout!" (11/1/80)
8. "The Abduction of Tom Sawyer" (11/8/80)
9. "The Silver Mine" (11/15/80)

10. "The Valley of Gold" (11/22/80)
11. "The Wildest Wild West Show" (11/29/80)
12. "The Black Mare" (12/6/80)
13. "The Renegade" (12/20/80)
14. "The Great Land Rush" (1/10/81)
15. "The Memory Trap" (1/17/81)
16. "The Runaway" (1/24/81)

ANIMATED SERIES EPISODES AND AIRDATES OF *THE TARZAN/LONE RANGER/ZORRO ADVENTURE HOUR*

Second Season

17. "Photo Finish" (9/19/81)
18. "Walk a Tight Wire" (9/26/81)
19. "High and Dry" (10/3/81)
20. "The Ghost Wagons" (10/10/81)
21. "The Great Train Treachery" (10/31/81)
22. "Blast-out" (11/7/81)
23. "Renegade Roundup" (11/21/81)
24. "Front Page Cover-up" (1/2/82)
25. "Unnatural Disaster" (1/9/82)
26. "Showdown on the Midnight Queen" (1/16/82)
27. "Banning's Raiders" (1/23/82)
28. "The Long Drive" (1/30/82)

The Tarzan/Lone Ranger Adventure Hour aired Saturdays from September 1980 to February 1981 at 12:30–1:30 p.m.; and from March 1981 to September 1981 at 10:00–11:00 a.m. Seen on Saturdays too until September 1982 was *The Tarzan/Lone Ranger/Zorro Adventure Hour*, as part of the daytime children's programming. *Tarzan* reruns were aired until 1984.

With the initial *The Lone Ranger* series in 1966, CBS's daytime programming chief Fred Silverman had championed its broadcast. The presentation of its villains and tales, while certainly of true comic book dimensions to compare even with titans DC and Marvel, was a reflection of the times. The shows from the early 1980s were reflective of *that* period.

However, the newer series' opening episode in 1980, "Hanga, the Night Monster," could just as easily have belonged to the earlier series. So could the eighth new episode, "The Abduction of Tom Sawyer," and its fictional character created by Mark Twain.

Differentiating themselves from the initial series, the later two animated shows downplayed the violent content; they even offered a little history lesson. A process called rotoscoping, the blending of live action movements with the animation, gave the newer shows a more realistic look.

Format Productions utilized the animation services of Halas and Batchelor for the 1966–69 series, plus another outfit, this one in Australia, Artransa Film Studios. Filmation was responsible for the art and animation on all its Lone Ranger and Tarzan adventures. While this studio also did the graphics and storyboards for Zorro, an outfit in Japan, Tokyo Movie Shinsha, did the latter's animating process.

No VHS tapes or DVDs were made available for the animated *Tarzan* shows, as the rights were part of the estate of the title character's creator, Edgar Rice Burroughs. However, the other animated heroes from the Filmation shows were put together on a pair of DVDs called *The New Adventures of the Lone Ranger and Zorro Volumes 1 & 2.*

Nine

The 1981 Film
The Legend of the Lone Ranger

The loyal friend he trusted.
The woman fate denied him.
The great silver stallion he rode.
And his consuming love of justice.
—tagline from the film's release

A Lord Grade and Jack Wrather Presentation. A Martin Starger Production. Released by Universal Pictures and Associated Film Distribution Corporation on May 22, 1981. 98 minutes. Panavision and Technicolor. Based on characters and stories created by George W. Trendle and Fran Striker.

Credits:
Producer: Walter Coblenz.
Executive Producer: Martin Starger.
Director: William A. Fraker.
Screenplay: Ivan Goff, Ben Roberts, Michael Kane, William Roberts.
Adaptation: Jerry Derloshon.
Photography: Laszlo Kovacs.
Editor: Thomas Stanford.
Production Designer: Albert Brenner.
Art Director: David M. Haber.
Set Decorator: Philip Abramson.
Makeup: William P. Turner.
Costume Designer: Noel Taylor.
Music: John Barry.

Cast:
Klinton Spilsbury (John Reid/The Lone Ranger); Michael Horse (Tonto); Christopher Lloyd (Bartholomew "Butch" Cavendish); Jason Robards (Ulysses S. Grant); Matt Clark (Sheriff Wiatt); Juanin Clay

132

(Amy Striker); John Bennett Perry (Dan Reid); David Hayward (Collins), John Hart (Lucas Striker); Richard Farnsworth (Wild Bill Hickok); Lincoln Tate (George A. Custer); Ted Flicker (Buffalo Bill Cody); Marc Gilpin (Young John Reid); Patrick Montoya (Young Tonto); Ted White (Jonathan Reid); Chere Bryson (Mrs. Reid); Merle Haggard (Balladeer); James Lee Crite, Jim Burke, Jeff Ramsey, Bennie Dobbins, Henry Wills, Greg Walker, Mike Adams, Ben Bates, Bill Hart, Larry Randles (Rangers); Robert Hoy, Ted Gehring, Buck Taylor, Tom R. Diaz, Chuck Hayward, Tom Laughlin, Terry Leonard, Steve Meador, Joe Finnegan, Roy Bonner, John M. Smith (Cavendish Gang).

Synopsis: In 1854 Texas, an Indian boy is saved from outlaws by a white boy. The boys are Tonto and John Reid. When John's parents are killed by the outlaws, he is taken to Tonto's Comanche village to live. Then his older brother Dan comes and sends John away to be raised by an aunt.

As a lawyer years later, John returns to Texas by stagecoach. The other passengers include a young lady, Amy Striker, whom he helps when outlaws try to rob the stage. Amy is the niece of the town of Del Rio's newspaper editor, Lucas Striker.

Outlaw leader Butch Cavendish's men are behind the robbery attempt. Two of them are turned over to Sheriff Wiatt, but he's another Cavendish man. The two prisoners become victims of a firing squad set up by Butch for having acted without orders.

John and Amy find themselves falling in love. Yet Lucas is hanged by Cavendish's orders for reporting about him in the newspaper. Now a Texas Ranger captain, Dan Reid and his men chase after Lucas's murderers. John rides along with his brother, who gives him a Ranger badge to make it official.

Collins, one of the Rangers, betrays his comrades by leading them into a trap in a canyon where they are gunned down by Butch Cavendish and his gang. Butch also has Collins wounded so the traitor will not be suspected of any duplicity.

John, still alive, is found by Tonto, who recognizes his blood brother by an amulet given to him when they were boys. Tonto helps John recover, and together they find the white stallion soon named Silver. With silver bullets given him by Tonto for accuracy, John's marksmanship with his guns becomes superior.

To avenge the killings by the Cavendish gang, John has an unfilled grave placed with the other Rangers so it will be believed he too was killed. Wearing a mask made from his dead brother's clothing, he becomes the Lone Ranger. When the masked man confronts Collins in the town saloon, the traitor is killed by a mysterious assailant. Sheriff Wiatt arrests Tonto as the Ranger escapes. When Wiatt lets townsfolk try to lynch the innocent Indian, the Lone Ranger rides to the rescue.

Cavendish and his outlaw gang kidnap President Ulysses S. Grant off a train. The Ranger and Tonto sneak into Butch's compound and free the president. Wiatt, also found there, is knocked unconscious by Tonto. Assisted by Grant, the Masked Man and his Indian companion rig dynamite charges to destroy the compound.

When the last dynamite blast breaks open the compound's gates, both Silver and Tonto's horse Scout lead the U.S. Cavalry in to help stop the outlaws. Cavendish tries to escape but the Lone Ranger chases after him. The outlaw leader is finally defeated in a fistfight. Although tempted to shoot his adversary down, the Ranger cannot condone the murder.

Cavendish is brought before President Grant for punishment. Grant promises Tonto that he will to try and honor the peace treaties with the Indians. As the Lone Ranger and Tonto ride off together, the President wonders just who *was* that masked man.

As early as 1975, Clayton Moore was told by the Wrather Corporation to stop making personal appearances as the Lone Ranger. The rights to the character were owned by Jack Wrather's company. At the time, Moore's personal appearances were how he was making a living. Moore and his agent Art Dorn sent a letter to the corporation stating that while the appearances would continue, Clayton would refrain from calling himself the Lone Ranger and instead be billed as the man who played the character.

This still did not satisfy the corporation and legal action was threatened unless Moore stopped altogether. Finally Clayton learned the reasoning behind all this: Wrather was preparing a new motion picture with a younger actor, *The Legend of the Lone Ranger*. Speaking with a Wrather attorney, Joel Boxer in 1979, Moore was told he was simply too old to continue his appearances.

Soon a restraining order was issued against Moore appearing in public wearing the mask. At an August 1979 hearing, Clayton attempted to reciprocate by showing that he was still in fit physical condition. But the presiding judge, Vernon Foster, had no recourse but to rule in favor of the Wrather Corporation since it did have the legal rights.

Dorn felt that Moore had every right to earn a living with the heroic figure that he had embodied for some 30 years via TV, films and

Following his years as the Lone Ranger on TV and in films, Clayton Moore continued to make personal appearances in character. In this shot, taken at a Rangers baseball game, he's on a horse he kept in Texas for these appearances.

public appearances. Moore agreed and began using wrap-around ski sunglasses, in addition to altering his costume a little, to continue with the appearances.

Fans accepted wholeheartedly the new look. Petitions circulated on his behalf all over the country had over a million signatures. In 1980, baseball's Texas Rangers and NBC-TV's audience participation series *Real People* supported Clayton. As Moore performed at their baseball games, the Rangers made him a mascot. On *Real People*, while Moore made a live appearance for an enthusiastic audience, a filmed segment also highlighted his personal appearances meeting his fans and signing autographs.

When the Wrather Corporation issued the injunction against Moore, his attorney Bob Michaels responded with a countersuit. The entire situation did not help Jack Wrather and Lord Grade, his production partner, with their chances of *The Legend of the Lone Ranger* becoming a box office hit.

Nor did it help the two companies, Associated Film and Universal Pictures, which released the film in May 1981. With $18,000,000 in production costs, the Western's $12,000,000 domestic gross showed it was a financial failure.

Lew Grade, or rather Lord Grade as he then called himself, was able through his own ITC Entertainment company to sell the television rights for $7,500,000.

In September 1984, litigation against Clayton Moore was dropped. In October, Bonita Granville Wrather sent Dorn a note which stated that Clayton was again free to wear the mask and appear in public as the Lone Ranger. Husband Jack Wrather may have had something to do with it, for he was suffering from the cancer which took his life only a few weeks later.

Wrather's production partner on the film was born as Louis Winogradsky in 1906. The name Lew Grade was first used when he was a professional dancer; in 1926, he was the World Charleston Champion.

Initial TV work for Grade was having ITC Entertainment produce the syndicated TV series *The Saint* in 1962. In 1969, he was knighted for his promotional work in international trade, and he became a baron in 1976 (hence the title Lord Grade). Perhaps he is best known in show business circles as the executive producer of the 1977 miniseries *Jesus of Nazareth* and 1979's *The Muppet Movie.* The great entrepreneur was 92 when he died in 1998.

Like Wrather and Grade, Martin Starger was an entertainment entrepreneur. Born in 1932, he was an executive producer on *The Muppet Movie* and a 1979 TV special, *The Muppets Go Hollywood.* Starger was a real creative force at ABC-TV during the 1970s. He had input on both the phenomenal *Happy Days* series and *Roots* miniseries. He later became president of Associated Film Distribution, which distributed the *Lone Ranger* film and all of Grade's ITC films.

The Legend of the Lone Ranger's producer, Walter Coblenz, was born in 1928. His career in entertainment began on television. Between 1961 and 1969, he was stage manager on the variety series *The Hollywood Palace.* In 1969, he was production manager on Robert Redford's *Downhill Racer.* He also produced two other Redford films, 1972's *The Candidate* and 1976's *All the President's Men.*

The director of the 1981 Western was William A. Fraker (1923–2010). He began his show business career in 1952 as a camera operator on the *Adventures of Ozzie and Harriet* TV show. Between 1956 and 1957, Fraker was the assistant cameraman on the *Lone Ranger* TV series. He received five Oscar nominations for his cinematography over the years. The first was for *Looking for Mr. Goodbar* in 1977. Fraker also directed three films, two of them Westerns: *Monte Walsh* in 1970 and *The Legend of the Lone Ranger.*

Four writers were credited for this *Lone Ranger* screenplay. Ivan Goff and Ben Roberts (longtime writing partners), Michael Kane and William Roberts. Yet another writer, Jerry Derloshon, was given a credit for adaptation.

Born in Australia in 1910, Goff began his writing career there on a newspaper. Ben Roberts, born in 1916 in New York City, initially wrote comedy for Broadway shows. In 1947, their professional collaboration began. Their joint screenplays included two with James Cagney, 1949's *White Heat* and 1957's *Man of a Thousand Faces.* The writing team created 109 TV episodes of the original *Charlie's Angels.* They also produced 169 episodes of the *Mannix* TV series between 1968 and 1975.

Roberts passed away in 1984 at age 68. Goff was 89 when he died from Alzheimer's in 1999.

No relation to Ben, William Roberts was born in 1913. He worked on the screenplays for two of the great Western classics, 1960s *The Magnificent Seven* and 1962's *Ride the High Country*. During the 1958–59 television season, Roberts was associate producer of *The Donna Reed Show*. Roberts died at 83 in 1997.

Michael Kane (a.k.a. Michael Joseph Kane) worked in both film and television. Other projects included *Smokey and the Bandit II*, a 1980 film, and the 1985 TV movie, *The Dirty Dozen: Next Mission*. Kane also directed episodes of *Gilligan's Island* and *The Brady Bunch*. He passed away in 2011 at age 88.

The Legend of the Lone Ranger gave credit to both George W. Trendle and Fran Striker as creators of the Lone Ranger stories and characters. Controversy between the two over just who was creator went on for years during their lifetime.

George Washington Trendle owned the radio station which aired the radio series for more than 20 years. A January 1933 letter from Trendle to Striker gave credit to the writer as creator; yet in the following year, Striker was pressured to sign over the rights. Their long association carried over into the TV series. Fran Striker (full name: Francis Hamilton Striker) reworked old scripts from the radio shows for use as TV episodes. In *Legend of the Lone Ranger*, the characters Amy Striker and Lucas Striker were named in the writer's honor.

By the time of the Western's release, Striker had been gone for more than 18 years. He was 59 when he was killed in a 1962 car accident. At 87, Trendle had died in 1972.

John Hart's good-natured and stalwart newspaperman is hanged rather abruptly by the bad element. Even more jarring is the dragging and shooting death of the young John Reid's mother, played by Chere Bryson.

Hart had the opportunity to reprise his Lone Ranger a few times after his original TV portrayal. In *The Phynx*, a 1970 feature, Hart and Jay Silverheels spoofed their famous roles. The movie was about a rock band which goes to the rescue of a whole group of show business folks from past years. This included Bowery Boys Leo Gorcey and Huntz Hall, Johnny (Tarzan) Weissmuller and Maureen (Jane) O'Sullivan. The Lone Ranger and Tonto were in on the proceedings too. Hart also appeared as the Masked Man in an April 1981 episode of *The Greatest American Hero* ("My Heroes Have Always Been Cowboys") and a February 1982 episode of *Happy Days* ("Hi Yo, Fonzie Away"). In the latter,

Fonzie (Henry Winkler) is celebrating a birthday and gets a chance to meet his personal hero, the Lone Ranger. Hart was 91 when he passed away in 2009.

When he was still in full swing as the Masked Man on the TV series, Clayton Moore spoofed his own image on The *Red Skelton Hour*. It was for a December 1955 segment of the comedy-variety television show, "Deadeye vs. the Lone Ranger." Sheriff Deadeye was the Skelton character.

During the 1960s, Moore and Jay Silverheels appeared in character on TV commercials for Geno's Pizza Rolls. Clayton also did TV ads for Aqua Velva After Shave. All the commercials were played with humor.

On a June 1979 TV special, and during the controversy over wearing the mask, Clayton was among the dozens of performers who appeared from past TV Western shows. Hosted by Glenn Ford and

John Hart as the Lone Ranger shakes hands with Henry Winkler's Fonzie as other *Happy Days* cast members look on.

dedicated to John Wayne, the program was called *When the West Was Fun: A Western Reunion*. The other performers included Chuck Connors and Johnny Crawford from *The Rifleman*, John Russell and Peter Brown from *Lawman* and James Drury and Doug McClure from *The Virginian*. Moore's Lone Ranger is first seen in the beginning when he walks into a bar tended by Larry Storch from *F Troop*. Apparently the special gave ABC its highest ratings of the year.

In 1982, Moore was inducted into the Stuntmen's Hall of Fame. The Cowboy Hall of Fame honored him in 1990 with its Western Heritage Award. The most beloved Lone Ranger of all died from a heart attack in December 1999. He was 85 years old.

Perhaps most rewarding of all for Clayton was the happy ending after all the fuss over the mask. Moore's mask was actually placed in Washington, D.C.'s Smithsonian Institution in 1985. Its Museum of American Culture recognized the mask as one of the 101 greatest objects of all time.

Klinton Spilsbury assuredly had more than a little weight on his shoulders living up to the Moore-Ranger persona for the 1981 film. He was born in 1950—the first season of the TV series. Clayton Moore thought that the handsome Spilsbury had the aura of a young Gary Cooper. The actor reminded me of a younger Gregory Peck, especially in the film's climactic fight with Christopher Lloyd's Butch Cavendish.

According to reports, Spilsbury became so arrogant over getting the role that it frustrated his co-workers. To make matters worse, problems with his voice during filming resulted in all his speaking lines being dubbed by fellow actor James Keach.

The Legend of the Lone Ranger was Klinton's first and last feature film appearance. His only prior acting roles were in 1978: billed as Max Keller, he appeared in a TV movie, *Suddenly, Love*, and on an episode of TV's *Lou Grant* series.

As Tonto, Michael Horse speaks perfect English. It is certainly a contrast to that spoken by Jay Silverheels. Horse, whose initial last name was Henrich, was born in 1951; he claimed to be of Native American descent, including Mescalero Apache. *Legend of the Lone Ranger* was his film debut.

Unlike Spilsbury, Horse's acting résumé was quite extensive. His many TV appearances included playing law enforcers on an episode of

Klinton Spilsbury as the masked hero in *The Legend of the Lone Ranger* (1981).

The X-Files in 1994 and in a recurring role on the *Twin Peaks* series during the 1990–91 season.

Michael Horse also had the burden of carrying a mythic character embodied by a beloved performer. Both younger men strive in the course of the film to capture the amiability yet fortitude of their predecessors. While the effort was not perfect, it was commendable.

My favorite sequence in the film with the two actors could have easily been part of the earlier television series. It is when Spilsbury's

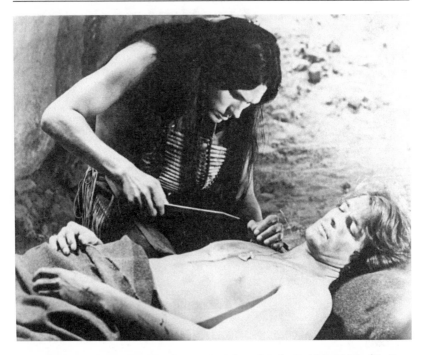

Michael Horse's Tonto saves Klinton Spilsbury's John Reid in 1981's *The Legend of the Lone Ranger.*

Lone Ranger, to the strains of the *William Tell Overture*, rides Silver into town to save Horse's Tonto from being lynched by Matt Clark's despicable sheriff.

In an earlier sequence, the *Overture* is heard as Klinton turns to face the camera and is seen wearing the mask for the first time; it actually brought laughs from the movie theater audience I was part of in 1981. The voice of both John Reid and his alter ego was indeed James Keach. But the dubbing is so well done that it is virtually impossible to detect.

Born in 1947, Keach is the younger brother of actor Stacy Keach. In the 1980 Western *The Long Riders*, James played outlaw Jesse James and Stacy his brother Frank.

Movie buffs will also remember James as the cop who stops Chevy Chase for tying the dog to the car bumper in 1984's *National Lampoon's Vacation*. He was married for many years to actress Jane Seymour.

Country singer Merle Haggard was the voice of the balladeer heard during the course of the *Lone Ranger* film. Over the opening credits he is heard singing the song "The Man in the Mask." The music was written by John Barry, the lyrics by Dean Pitchford. All in all, a nice attempt to add to the title character's mystique.

The most distinguished actor in the film was Jason Robards. While not looking much like the real President Grant, Robards still made the character seem like a real man. No small feat for a film with the storybook allure of the Lone Ranger.

Born in 1922 as Jason Nelson Robards, Jr., he won a Tony Award, an Emmy and a pair of Academy Awards. He was the voice of Grant in a 1990 television miniseries documentary, *The Civil War*. Robards also portrayed Abraham Lincoln in three TV movies: *Abe Lincoln in Illinois* (1964), *The Perfect Tribute* (1991) and—voice only—*Lincoln* (1992). The actor died at the age of 78 in December 2000.

Seen all too briefly in *Legend of the Lone Ranger* was actress Juanin Clay. As our hero's love interest Amy Striker, she was radiant. But the writers simply leave her character bravely carrying on her uncle's newspaper work and she is sorely missed during the rest of the film.

Born in 1949, Juanin was in contention for the female lead in 1979 for the *Buck Rogers in the 25th Century* TV series. She did get to play another role on two episodes of the series in both 1979 and 1980. She had a regular role in the 1976–77 TV season on the daytime soap opera *The Edge of Night*. In the 1985 television miniseries *Robert Kennedy and His Times*, she portrayed Jacqueline Kennedy.

The finest performance to come out of the *Lone Ranger* film might be that of John Bennett Perry. His was an honest portrayal of Dan Reid, the Texas Ranger captain, weathered and wearied by his responsibilities.

Born in 1941 the actor's TV work over the years included a regular role on the 1979–81 series *240-Robert*. In the TV movie *I Married Wyatt Earp* (1983), he was the hero's nemesis John Behan. Many may remember Perry as the sailor from the Old Spice TV commercials in the 1970s.

He is the father of actor Matthew Perry; over the years they have enjoyed working together, including a 2004 episode of the younger Perry's television series *Scrubs*.

Born in 1938, Christopher Lloyd's first film was *One Flew Over the Cuckoo's Nest* (1975), playing a mental patient. A better actor would be hard to find portraying more characters on the fringe between lunacy and sanity, and as both good guys and bad guys. Perhaps Lloyd's most recognized role was the lovable nutcase the "Reverend" Jim, one of the cabbies, on the *Taxi* TV series. Another of his good guy roles was the fruity inventor in the *Back to the Future* films starting in 1985. Lloyd's colorful villains were always interesting too; and this included the Klingon commander in 1984's *Star Trek III: The Search for Spock* and Major Bartholomew "Butch" Cavendish in *The Legend of the Lone Ranger*.

While Lloyd's Cavendish was played with a ramrod straight military bearing, never concealed was the twisted, murderous bent to forge a frontier empire. Any actual over-the-top theatrics, however, were supplied by his wild bunch of henchmen. Three henchmen stand out during the stagecoach hold up at the beginning of the film: Ted Gehring's Stillwell, Buck Taylor's Gattlin and Terry Leonard's Valentine.

Theodore Edwin "Ted" Gehring Jr. was born in 1929. A prolific character actor, his many TV Western appearances included eight *Bonanza*s between 1968 and 1972 and five *Gunsmoke*s between 1966 and 1973. His threatening yet amusing bad guy in *Lone Ranger* is noticed when he opens the stagecoach door and, even through his hooded disguise, marvels wide-eyed at the plunder. At the age of 71, Gehring died in September 2000.

Also disguised in a hood, the varmint played by Buck Taylor makes lascivious eyes at Amy. Buck was born in 1938 as Walter Clarence Taylor III. He is the son of noted character actor Dub Taylor. Between 1967 and 1975, Buck was seen on 174 episodes of the *Gunsmoke* series. Most were as blacksmith and sometimes deputy Newly O'Brien. He reprised the role in the 1987 TV movie *Gunsmoke: Return to Dodge*.

In 1981, stuntman-actor Terry Leonard performed a pair of thrilling stunts that are among the greatest of all time. They were for *The Legend of the Lone Ranger* and *Raiders of the Lost Ark*. And the stunts were a tribute to Yakima Canutt's similar work on 1939's *Stagecoach*.

Leonard's own work on the *Ranger* film has him, like Yak years earlier, jumping onto the stage's running horses and then falling beneath them as the coach passes over. In reality, it ran over Terry and he spent three months recuperating.

Other henchmen in the Western included Robert F. Hoy and Tom Laughlin. Hoy's Perlmutter is Butch Cavendish's right hand man. Laughlin, who played the character Neeley, was quite well known for hero Billy Jack in a few films between 1967 and 1977.

Playing Collins, the traitorous Texas Ranger actually in cahoots with the Cavendish gang, was David Hayward. He began his acting career on a 1969 episode of the *Adam-12* TV series. A few regular roles on television followed for Hayward: they included both the *Knots Landing* series in the 1988–89 season and *Beverly Hills 90210* in the 1994–95 season.

Clearly the traitor's conscience troubles him in the Western as he is found drunk in a saloon by the Ranger. The unseen assailant who guns Collins down just may be Matt Clark's Sheriff Wiatt, whose conscience bothers *him* not a bit. Clark, who was born in 1936, had his first TV role on a 1964 episode of the *Ben Casey* series. His initial Western feature was as one of the Quints terrorizing Charlton Heston in 1967's *Will Penny*. Always a plus in a Western, Clark was seen in at least five of them (including *The Cowboys* and *Jeremiah Johnson*) in 1972. In the *Ranger* film, Clark's true skunk is last seen getting knocked cold by Tonto—a justifiable act in light of the earlier situation when the noble Indian was framed for murder.

"The visual beauty of the movie is no surprise since the director— William A. Fraker—is one of the most brilliant cinematographers in Hollywood, and his cinematographer—Laszlo Kovacs—is also a champion." This from a review by the *Christian Science Monitor* in May 1981.

"But credit must be shared with the locations they have used," continued the *Monitor*. Actually, over a dozen were utilized for the Western. They included parts of Monument Valley in both Utah and Arizona, and Bronson Canyon and Vasquez Rocks Natural Area Park in California. The New Mexico locations were the Eaves Movie Ranch and the Cumbres & Toltec Scenic Railroad.

The writers of the Western certainly stuck with the tried-and-true in the origin story of the group of Texas Rangers being ambushed in Bryant's Gap Canyon. The first portion of the film goes all the way back to the TV series roots with the meeting of the young Tonto and John Reid (here played by Patrick Montoya and Marc Gilpin).

In the 1950s TV series, Silver is initially found injured. For the film, Silver is first seen by Tonto and the Lone Ranger trapped in a ravine.

Klinton Spilsbury and Michael Horse on their own Silver and Scout in this scene from 1981's *The Legend of the Lone Ranger*.

Lord Grade, after the film's release, said the reason the movie failed "was not dispensing with the legend in ten minutes and getting on with the action much earlier on." The *New York Times* opined, "An hour into the film, the *William Tell Overture* is finally played and the audience wakes up as one. From that point on, *The Legend of the Lone Ranger* is standard, halfhearted adventure fare."

Perhaps Clayton Moore's own concept for a scenario might have better served the producers' interests. He had Tonto dead and the Masked Man mentoring a young man on the fence between good and evil. Together they fight the forces of evil with the Ranger then turning the mask over to the younger man.

A very nostalgic moment occurs at the end of *The Legend of the Lone Ranger*, when longtime radio and television announcer Fred Foy is again heard heralding our hero. Foy died of natural causes in December 2010. He was 89.

Foy had fond memories of radio's Brace Beemer taking his Lone Ranger persona into hospitals to cheer up children. Beemer died at age 62 in 1965. While Klinton Spilsbury was adept in conveying the character's spirit in the film, there were reports of his not always being cooperative doing publicity stints. In any case, he did not have the same opportunity Beemer and Moore had, to continue playing the Lone Ranger over a long period of time.

Ten

The 2003 TV Movie
The Lone Ranger

I couldn't have done it without you.
—The Lone Ranger to Tonto

A Warner Bros. Television and Turner Network Television Presentation. Originally Broadcast on the WB Network on February 26, 2003. 120 minutes. Color.

Credits:
Producer: Mel Efros.
Executive Producers: Eric Ellenbogen, Kate Jurgens.
Director: Jack Bender.
Writers: Jonathan Penner, Stacy Title.
Photography: Steven Fierberg.
Editors: Luis Colina, Mark Melnick.
Production Designer: Sandy Veneziano.
Costume Designer: Karyn Wagner.
Makeup: Lisa Rocco
Music: Roger Neill.

Cast:
Chad Michael Murray (Luke Hartman/The Lone Ranger); Nathaniel Arcand (Tonto); Wes Studi (Kulakinah); Dylan Walsh (Kansas City Haas); Anita Brown (Alope); Fay Masterson (Grace Hartman); Sebastian Spence (Harmon Hartman); Jeffrey Nordling (James Landry); Gil Birmingham (One Horn); Paul Schulze (Sheriff Landry); Bradford Tatum (Tryon); Lauren German (Emily Landry); Tod Thawley (Tera); Mike Weinberg (Harmon Jr.); Sam Hennings (Luke's Father).

Synopsis: Luke Hartman, a young Boston law student, travels by stagecoach to a town out West. His brother Harmon has a trading post there with wife Grace and their son Harmon Jr. The elder Harmon is

148

also leader of the Texas Rangers. When another Texas Ranger, Kansas City Haas, alerts Harmon about the threatening element known as the Regulators, all the Rangers ride after them. Told to stay behind, Luke soon joins his brother on the trail. Harmon is impressed by the younger man's uncanny skill with a gun. While camped, Haas reveals himself as the Regulators' leader and they shoot down Harmon and the other Rangers. Luke, wounded, is left for dead.

Saved by the Apache Tonto, Luke is taken to his village. There Luke is also cared for by Alope, Tonto's sister, and the tribe's spiritual guide Kulakinah. Although Luke only wants to kill Kansas City Haas, Kulakinah and Tonto help him instead to find his spiritual well-being. Alope brings Luke the stallion Silver as part of his spiritual quest. Tonto teaches him to better defend himself. Following these rites of passage, Luke is called Kemo Sabe by Tonto for their friendship. Kulakinah gives Luke a mask to wear to bring fear to his enemies.

Chief One Horn, Tera and other Apaches do not want to become involved with Luke's battle against Haas and the Regulators. Town businessman James Landry and its sheriff are both in cahoots with the Regulators to drive the settlers off their land for the railroad.

As Haas and his men burn out a frontier family, Luke appears as the Masked Man to stop them. Silver prevents Luke from shooting Haas down in cold blood.

Friction between Tonto and his fellow Apaches continues over his support for Luke against the Regulators. When the sheriff is sent by Landry to confront Haas over the delay in getting rid of both the settlers and Indians, Kansas City murders him.

As Tonto and the Ranger use blasting material taken from the trading post against the Regulators, Luke saves his own friend's life. Tera and other Indians now also help the two in their struggle.

The Regulators are defeated. Again having the chance to kill Haas, Luke stops himself but is forced to wound him. James Landry's deception seems unnoticed by others in town, even by his daughter Emily. Luke decides to stay on and help care for his sister-in-law and nephew. Kulakinah gives Luke his brother's Texas Ranger badge to reflect that he is now the Lone Ranger.

Tonto and the Lone Ranger ride off together for further adventures.

Chad Michael Murray attempted to revamp the Masked Man for the 2003 TV movie *The Lone Ranger*.

Upon the capture of villainous Kansas City Haas in this TV movie, the Lone Ranger's response is a bit startling: "You'll rot in jail," he states, "and Hell ain't goin' anywhere."

This quote does not sound like a comment from a Boston lawyer, nor from the Lone Ranger we all remember the most. Clayton Moore always seemed to speak with such perfect diction, yet the Masked Man's identity was, of course, John Reid, not Chad Michael Murray's Luke Hartman.

While similarities with both characters remained the same (mask and steed Silver for example), this time there is no white hat for our hero nor silver bullets for his gun belt. But not to worry in the latter regard for he is a naturally skilled marksman.

Seen too was the killing of the Texas Rangers, especially defenseless bedded down in their camp. Instead of both Butch Cavendish and Collins as the treacherous foes, Kansas City Haas functions as the catalyst of evil for this adventure.

Of special interest in the 2003 version were the Indian portrayals. They are given a colorful if more modern twist. This is seen not only with Nathaniel Arcand's kung fu-fighting Tonto, but with some sexual excitement from the Indian's own sister Alope, played by Anita Brown.

The 1981 feature had showed a romantic angle between John Reid and Amy Striker, but it was more sublimely handled. While Alope and Luke Hartman do share a nude scene in a hot spring, it is revealed as being envisioned by the latter as part of his spiritual quest. Luke also envisions his dead brother and father.

Alope and another leading Indian character, Wes Studi's Kulaki-nah, were new to the Lone Ranger legend. Yet the mysticism generated by the latter was completely in keeping with the spirituality sought by young Hartman.

In any event, this version was definitely meant to reflect a hipper, cooler Lone Ranger specifically for teenage and twentysomething viewers. This was felt right down to the rock music credited to Roger Neill. Even when the *William Tell Overture* is finally heard at the end of the movie, it is performed with an electric guitar to jazz it up.

Initially aired on the WB Network in February 1903, the movie was an attempt by Warner Brothers Television and Turner Television to create a new series. It failed to connect with the younger audience it was intended for. "Talk about a disaster," wrote one online reviewer. "I'm not talking about the actors (who did a good job with what they had). I'm talking writing."

Certainly emphasis regarding the writing was on changing the origins of the Lone Ranger in the hopes of sustaining new interest. Yet just as certainly, this was a no-no for some viewers. But the husband-

and-wife writing team Jonathan Penner and Stacy Title must be commended for their sincere attempts to give the old tale a fresh viewpoint.

What I found especially interesting from the writers was Tonto's being torn by his conflicting loyalties to both his tribe and Luke Hartman. It makes for some compelling and anxious moments.

Writers Title and Penner were also the executive producers. A 1999 film they worked on in both categories was *Let the Devil Wear Black*. On *Bye Bye Man* (2016) they teamed again; this time Jonathan was the sole writer and Stacy the director.

Producer Mel Efros also produced 14 episodes of the TV series *Lois and Clark: The New Adventures of Superman* in 1993 and 1994. He was also co-producer of the 1989 feature, *Star Trek V: The Final Frontier*.

Along with his chores as an executive producer on the TV movie, Eric Ellenbogen performed that duty for the 2013 feature *The Lone Ranger*. Born in 1957, the last year of the fabled TV series, he also executive-produced the 2014–15 series *The New Adventures of Lassie*.

In 2002, just before her stint with *The Lone Ranger* TV movie, Kate Juergens produced a program called *Hidden Hills*. She also served as a network executive on other television programs, including *Lincoln Heights* between 2004 and 2008.

Susanne Daniels was executive producer on 16 episodes of a 2008 TV series, *How to Look Good Naked*. She was also given an online credit as executive producer on this Ranger project.

Having his hands full directing 2003's *Lone Ranger* adventure was Jack Bender. Yet he too made a sincere and earnest effort. He was born in 1949, the first year of the original TV show. Initially an actor, he appeared in such favorite TV series of the 1970s as *The Bob Newhart Show* and *The Mary Tyler Moore Show*.

But it was as a director that Bender was most proficient, working in series programming and TV movies. The latter included 1990's *The Dreamer of Oz*. Bender was both director and executive producer on 38 episodes of the cult series *Lost* between 2004 and 2010, including the much-anticipated final episode.

"The Lone Ranger's costume was pretty lousy," said another online review of the TV movie. The dark hat, shirt and pants just did not fit well the memories of our beloved hero. (As if Chad Michael Murray did not have *enough* challenges to face with his boyish looks and lanky frame.) Still his performance was just fine and he had a likable presence.

Born in 1981, the year Klinton Spilsbury's version came out, Murray was just 21 when he portrayed the Lone Ranger. Had the movie become a series and he was given a more suitable outfit to wear, the actor may have grown into the role and made a better impression. There was a warm rapport between Murray and both Sebastian Spence (who played his brother) and Nathaniel Arcand.

One of my favorite scenes is when Luke shows concern over Tonto's nearly being drowned by two Regulators during the climax. The bond realized here was touching.

As an actor, Murray initially made his mark on the WB Network series *Gilmore Girls* (2000–01) and *Dawson's Creek* (2001–02). It was in 131 episodes of the WB's *One Tree Hill* TV series that he really made an impression with younger viewers between 2003 and 2012.

Nathaniel Arcand's performance as Tonto may have been the strongest one in *The Lone Ranger.* And I say this not to take away from either Murray or Wes Studi, the latter one of the most recognized actors

Chad Michael Murray's hero and Nathaniel Arcand's Tonto—and Silver and Scout—in 2003's *The Lone Ranger.*

to portray Indian roles. An exceptional performer, Arcand was born in 1971. In his blood ran Plains Cree Indian ancestry. He made his mark with his first major TV series, *North of 60*, between 1994 and 1997.

As with Studi, a number of Indian roles were part of Arcand's acting career. Two prominent ones were in a 2010 film, *Two Indians Talking*, and on nine episodes of a 2011 TV series called *Blackstone*. The latter's setting was a Plains Cree community.

A native Cherokee, Wes Studi was born in 1947. In the early 1990s, he appeared in two of his strongest Indian roles, as Magua in *The Last of the Mohicans* and in the title role of *Geronimo: An American Legend*. Never was there a more fierce warrior than his Magua, but Studi balanced his Indian portrayals with a gentler side. Such was the case with the 1999 miniseries *Streets of Laredo* and 2003's *The Lone Ranger*. Kulakinah, his wise old spiritual guide, seemed perfect for lighting our young masked hero's trail. Studi's presence added even more dignity to the role.

Anita Brown's Alope was another interesting new character added to the Lone Ranger legend. With her gracefulness and beauty, she seemed the epitome of every Indian princess seen on films or television. It's surprising that the actress has not made a greater impact. One of her first TV appearances was on a 2001 episode of *Dark Angel*. She also made two appearances on the *Supernatural* series, one episode in 1905 and another in 1908.

Sebastian Spence is remembered for his role as "Cowboy" Cliff Harting on the TV series *Cedar Cove* (29 episodes between 2013 and 2015). In both American and Canadian television over the years, the actor's credits are extensive. In 2002 he had a recurring role on *Dawson's Creek*, the same series which featured Chad Michael Murray. As Harmon Hartman, Luke's brother, Sebastian reminded me right away of John Bennett Perry's Dan Reid from the prior *Lone Ranger* film. Both had amiable and winning personalities.

For the 2003 movie, the brother's having a wife and son added more interest. Fay Masterson and Mike Weinberg conveyed well the heartbreak shared by Grace and Harmon Jr. over the loss of Harmon.

For most of the TV movie, Tod Thawley seemed like the stereotypical Indian bent on villainy. Not just at odds, like Gil Birmingham's chief, over whether Tonto should be supported in his friendship with Luke, Thawley's Tera had a hatred for all white men. Only at the last moment does the Apache relent and join Tonto and the Ranger against their enemies.

Born in 1971, Thawley appeared on episodes of *Baywatch* and *Walker, Texas Ranger* in 1996. He was also seen on three episodes of another hit series, *ER*, between 1999 and 2001.

During the TV movie, Tod's Apache and fellow tribesmen are interested in buying guns from Dylan Walsh's Kansas City Haas, who would backstab them along with everyone else in his way. Born Charles Hunter Walsh, the actor (born in 1963) was billed as such on his first TV series, *Kate & Allie*, in which he had a recurring role between 1987 and 1989. The year of his *Lone Ranger* appearance, he also began playing Dr. Sean McNamara on the *Nip/Tuck* series. He appeared in 100 episodes until 2010. Between 2011 and 2016, the versatile actor had a regular role on yet another television series, *Unforgettable*.

Paul Schulze, who played Sheriff Landry, was born in 1962. He appeared in recurring and regular TV roles on series programming. The first in this regard was *Oz* in 1998. On *The Sopranos*, between 1999 and 2006, the actor appeared in 13 episodes as Father Phil Intintola. Between 2009 and 2015, Schulze was on 80 episodes of *Nurse Jackie.*

Among those threatening Tonto in the climactic battle was Bradford Tatum's Tryon. As one of the Regulators, he supplied the appropriate menace. Tatum was born in 1965. One of his early TV roles was in the *Hunter* series in 1990. It was a two-parter and he was billed as Brad Tatum. The actor appeared in eight episodes each of two other shows as a recurring character. They were *The Burning Zone* in 1997 and *Magic City* in 2012.

The liberties taken by those involved on this *Lone Ranger* production, while showing promise at times, only seemed to irk die-hard fans of the original TV show. Few or none wanted the story of John Reid replaced or forgotten. Yet the alteration more than likely had to do with the poor response to the 1981 film, which had more or less stuck to the Reid origins. When viewed fairly, as I have attempted, the good intentions by those involved on the 2003 movie cannot be overlooked.

But kung fu fighting, Indians with perfect knowledge of the English language, and a pair of young heroes riding for a audience of their peers was not what the older fans wanted. Those who had grown up with Clayton Moore and Jay Silverheels, including myself, did not want to let that nostalgia go.

Eleven

The 2013 Film
The Lone Ranger

Horse says you are a spirit walker.
A man who's been to the other side and returned.
A man who cannot be killed in battle.
—Tonto to John Reid

A Disney and Jerry Bruckheimer Presentation. A Blind Wink/ Infinitum Nihil Production. A Gore Verbinski Film. Released by Walt Disney Studios Motion Pictures on July 3, 2013. 149 minutes. Color.

Credits:
Producers: Jerry Bruckheimer, Gore Verbinski.
Executive Producers: Johnny Depp, Eric Ellenbogen, Ted Elliott, Eric McLeod, Chad Oman, Terry Rossio, Mike Stenson.
Director: Gore Verbinski.
Screen Story and Screenplay: Ted Elliott, Justin Haythe, Terry Rossio.
Photography: Bojan Bozelli.
Editors: James Haygood, Craig Wood.
Production Designers: Jess Gonchor, Crash McCreery.
Visual Effects Supervisors: Tim Alexander, Gary Brozenich.
Costume Designer: Penny Rose.
Music: Hans Zimmer.

Cast:
Johnny Depp (Tonto); Armie Hammer (John Reid/The Lone Ranger); Tom Wilkinson (Latham Cole); William Fichtner (Butch Cavendish); Barry Pepper (Captain Jay Fuller); James Badge Dale (Dan Reid); Ruth Wilson (Rebecca Reid); Helena Bonham Carter (Red Harrington); Leon Rippy (Collins); Stephen Root (Habberman); Harry Treadaway (Frank); Robert Baker (Navarro); Gil Birmingham (Red Knee); Joaquin Casio (Jesus); James Frain (Barret); Saginaw Grant (Chief Big Bear); Damon Herriman (Ray), Matt O'Leary (Skinny); Lew Temple (Hollis);

Mason Cook (Will); Steve Corona (Young Cole); Joseph Foy (Boy Tonto); Travis Hammer (Young Cavendish); Bryant Prince (Danny Reid).

Synopsis: At a 1933 fair, a little boy, Will, is wearing a mask like his hero the Lone Ranger. Meeting the old Comanche Tonto, who is part of the Wild West Exhibition, Will is told an incredible story.

Lawyer John Reid is traveling back to Texas in 1869 on the Transcontinental Railroad. Also aboard the train are Texas Ranger prisoners Tonto and Butch Cavendish, the latter an outlaw en route to a hanging. Tonto's crime apparently is being an Indian.

While Tonto and John try to prevent Butch from getting away, his gang does free him. Dan Reid, John's Texas Ranger brother, chases after the Cavendish gang with his own men. John is deputized as a Ranger.

Following Collins, a traitorous Ranger, the other

Publicity shots of Johnny Depp and Armie Hammer for 2013's *The Lone Ranger.*

Rangers are ambushed by the outlaw gang. Having escaped from jail, Tonto finds the dead men and buries them. Spirit horse Silver appears to help save John, who then wears a mask to protect his identity while he avenges the killings.

Tonto and the Masked Man learn from Red Harrington, a brothel madam, that Collins and Dan had quarreled over a mysterious hunk of silver. Dan's wife Rebecca and their boy Danny are attacked by "Comanche Indians"—actually members of the Cavendish gang.

Regretting his treachery, Collins tries to help Rebecca and Danny when their lives are threatened by Butch. Railroad tycoon Latham Cole intervenes and kills Collins. Cole then has Captain Fuller and his cavalry go after actual Comanches.

The Indians find John and Tonto and bury them up to their necks in the dirt. Apparently Tonto is an outcast from the tribe: Years earlier, he had been duped into helping Cavendish and Cole murder tribal members for information about a mountain of silver. After Fuller and his soldiers ride past, Silver helps free John, who in turn frees Tonto.

At the silver mountain, Butch is captured by John and Tonto. When Tonto threatens the outlaw's life, John must knock his friend unconscious. Cavendish is turned over to Cole and Fuller.

John discovers that Cole and Cavendish are partners in the silver mine; and Fuller is also implicated. A military execution is soon being planned for John.

Tonto comes to John's rescue in the nick of time. Meanwhile, the Comanches are cut down by Fuller and his men.

Using the silver, Cole's plans are to seize control of the railroad. In an effort to stop him, the Masked Man and Tonto blow up a railroad bridge. Also trying to stop Cole, Red Harrington assists Tonto in stealing the train carrying the silver.

The Lone Ranger and Tonto find themselves on separate trains running parallel, although Tonto's is going backwards. With Silver's help, the Ranger rescues Rebecca from Butch's clutches. Danny makes his way to one of the engines.

Separating the other train cars from the one that Cavendish is in, the Ranger sends him to a high-speed doom (a collision with another detached train section). Fuller is also killed.

As the Masked Man stops Cole from shooting Tonto, the railroad man is trapped on a section of the train with the silver. He plummets to his own death off the previously destroyed bridge. All the silver is lost in the river far below.

After being congratulated by the railroad and saving his goodbyes to Rebecca (who has always loved him) and Danny, John rides away with Tonto at his side. John Reid is indeed now the Lone Ranger.

As the story returns to 1933, and Will questions its truth, Tonto hands him a silver bullet. Tonto walks away and becomes part of a Western landscape.

Columbia Pictures had planned a *Lone Ranger* feature film before the TV movie aired. A female Tonto was suggested by the studio. The writing team of David and Janet Peoples was involved on the screenplay during 2003. The rewriting process was the responsibility of Laeta Kalogridis.

In 2004, Jonathan Mostow was slated to direct. A $70,000,000 budget was set. But then the project fell through.

Classic Media owned the feature film rights at the time and had

Johnny Depp and Armie Hammer in the 2013 reload of *The Lone Ranger*.

made the initial arrangement with Columbia Pictures. Entertainment Rights, acquiring Classic Media, picked up the option in 2007 and worked out a joint arrangement involving Jerry Bruckheimer and the Walt Disney Company. This resulted in another writing team being brought in, Ted Elliott and Terry Rossio. The rewriting this time was done by Justin Haythe.

Johnny Depp got involved in 2008 when he agreed to play Tonto. With his production company, Infinitum Nihil, involved as well, he became one of the film's executive producers.

Director Gore Verbinski came aboard in 2010. Eric Ellenbogen, involved in this production and the TV movie, was one of the founders of an outfit called Boomerang Media. It apparently took over the interests in Entertainment Rights, unifying them into a subsidiary again called Classic Media. Ellenbogen had been a founder of the initial Classic Media in 2000.

But in 2012, DreamWorks Animation acquired the Classic Media subsidiary from Boomerang. Ellenbogen was also a founder of DreamWorks Animation's subsidiary, DreamWorks Classics. The catalog of titles in the transition from Classic Media included the *Lone Ranger* TV show.

In yet another turn of events, NBC Universal acquired DreamWorks Animation and its subsidiary in April 2016. If any of this seems confusing, it is understandable.

In March 2012, a decade after the first planning of *The Lone Ranger*, filming commenced. The movie was shot in Arizona, California, Colorado, New Mexico, Texas and Utah. Among the magnificent vistas seen were the fabled Monument Valley on the Utah-Arizona border and New Mexico's Cimarron Canyon State Park. Second unit work utilized the parking lot of California's Santa Anita Racetrack.

Among the very special features of the film were the trains and railway used. Near Albuquerque, New Mexico, a huge oval track was built to accommodate the two steam locomotives and assorted train cars. A half dozen railroad locations were used.

The locomotive seen at the beginning of *The Lone Ranger* later turned up as part of the Constitution train in the exciting climax. My favorite part of the movie is when our hero rides Silver atop the moving train cars to the accompaniment of the *William Tell Overture*. The train was going about 30 miles per hour.

Gandy Dancer Railroad and Excavating Services were responsible for all the rail work. The locomotives were built in a Sun Valley, California, machine shop. Special effects produced the steam and smoke coming from both engines.

The film's marvelous visual effects, created by Industrial Light & Magic, were nominated for an Academy Award. Another Oscar nomination was for Best Makeup and Hairstyling.

Nicknamed "Mr. Blockbuster," producer Jerry Bruckheimer's films have earned over $13 billion. He was honored by *Variety* magazine in 2003 as the first Hollywood producer to have the two top films in a single weekend, *Bad Boys II* and *Pirates of the Caribbean: The Curse of the Black Pearl.*

Jerome Leon Bruckheimer was born in 1943. As a producer he enjoyed great success on television with such shows as *CSI Crime Scene Investigation* and *CSI: Miami.* From 2004 to 2009, Bruckheimer had a total of six hit TV shows on the air.

Lone Ranger co-producer and director Gore Verbinski was born with the first name of Gregor in 1964. With Bruckheimer producing, Verbinski's film work as a director included the initial three *Pirates of the Caribbean* features. The third *Pirates* caper, *At World's End*, was the third film in history to make over $1 billion. Verbinski's initial film as a director was 1997's *Mouse Hunt*. His first film with his Blind Wink Productions, 2011's *Rango*, earned Verbinski an Oscar for Best Animated Feature.

Ted Elliott and Terry Rossio's teamwork as writers also included five *Pirates of the Caribbean* movies between 2003 and 2017. They also worked on *The Mask of Zorro* in 1998 and *The Legend of Zorro* in 2005. Rossio was born in 1960, Elliott a year later. They won an Academy Award (Writing Adapted Screenplay) for 2005's animated feature *Shrek*. One of their first film collaborations was on the animated *Aladdin* (1992).

Justin Haythe was born in 1973. His novel *The Honeymoon* was a nominee for the 2004 Man Booker Prize. Also in 2004, he wrote the screenplay for his most successful film thus far, *The Clearing*. When Haythe helped to rewrite the *Lone Ranger* story, he supposedly had to deal with a more supernatural element including ghost coyotes and even werewolves. In any case, the *Ranger* story and script by all three writers was criticized for being uneven.

One thing's for certain, the influx of gags written for the film proved amusing as well as annoying. In particular were those involving the Ranger's steed, Silver. In one instance, Silver is seen by our two main heroes wearing the Lone Ranger's white hat. In another scene, the horse burps after drinking a bottle of beer.

Early on, when the wounded John is pulled along on the travois by Tonto riding Silver, John's head is dragging on the ground right over the horse's droppings. At the farm attacked by the Indian imposters, Silver mysteriously appears on a rooftop. "The horse can fly?" asks John. "Don't be stupid," retorts Tonto.

My favorite gag occurs at the end when the Lone Ranger bellows, "Hi-Yo Silver! Away!" A startled Tonto then snaps back, "Don't ever do that again." When William Fichtner's evil Butch Cavendish drops Ruth Wilson's heroine, Rebecca Reid, off the moving train, she lands backwards on Silver. The Ranger then suddenly drops down on the saddle to face her in a suggestive, intimate way. She slaps him, then kisses him.

Depp's mystical Indian is a real hoot, from the beginning when he appears like a mannequin in the Wild West Exhibition, to the very end when the stuffed black bird he wears as part of his headgear seemingly comes to life and flies away. Despite his facial war paint making him appear a bit clownish, the performer's Tonto is also fearsome and loyal.

The role of Tonto offered Depp another opportunity to showcase his wonderful versatility. He was born John Christopher Depp II in 1963. Perhaps his greatest legacy as an actor is the role of Captain Jack Sparrow in the five *Pirates of the Caribbean* films right up to 2017's *Dead Men Tell No Tales.*

But Depp's list of film roles are impressive in any shape or form. They include vampire Barnabas Collins in *Dark Shadows*, Willy Wonka in 2005's *Charlie and the Chocolate Factory* and the title role in 1990's *Edward Scissorhands.*

Depp's *Lone Ranger* co-star Armie Hammer was impressive as well. Born Armand Douglas Hammer in 1986, he landed early TV roles on episodes of *Arrested Development* in 2005 and *Veronica Mars* in 2006. In 2009, he began playing recurring characters on two TV shows: Gabriel Edwards on four episodes of *Gossip Girl* and Morgan on five episodes of *Reaper.* In 2015, he played Illya in the *Man from U.N.C.L.E.*

film. He also voiced the Lone Ranger on several video games between 2013 and 2015.

In the *Lone Ranger* film, Hammer and Depp had a fine rapport. Armie's facial features even bore a slight resemblance to Clayton Moore's despite the drawback of sometimes needing a shave. Another drawback was having to wear a suit coat in the role, I guess because the character's background was as a lawyer. (Klinton Spilsbury too was a lawyer in the 1981 feature, but he wore a more traditional outfit as the Ranger.) Hammer certainly would have looked better without the coat. His familiar white hat and dark mask seen were well in keeping with the character's origins.

James Badge Dale's Dan Reid seemed to be cut from the mold of a Wyatt Earp: gritty, resolute, even sporting a handlebar mustache. Dan is handy too with a bullwhip, but less handy with his wife Rebecca. There's a strain in the marriage as Dan seems devoted more to his duties as a Texas Ranger; also, there is a hint of an attraction between her and John when they see each other after his return to the West.

Undoubtedly because fans all know what his fate will be, the Ranger's brother has always been a sympathetic character. It is made more true here due to his young son's devotion to him. Little Danny, played by Bryant Prince, conveys this bond quite nicely.

Born in 1978, Dale began his film career as a child actor with the role of Simon in 1990's *Lord of the Flies*. He later played roles on a few of producer Bruckheimer's TV series, including serial killer Henry Darius on two separate 2005 shows, *CSI: Miami* and *CSI: NY*.

Lone Ranger heroines Ruth Wilson and Helena Bonham Carter were both born in England. Wilson was especially prolific on television. Her breakthrough part was the title role in the 2006 miniseries *Jane Eyre*, for which she received a Golden Globe nomination. She later won a Golden Globe as Best Actress in a Drama Series for playing Allison Bailey on 22 episodes of *The Affair* during the 2014–15 TV season.

Bonham Carter's very impressive film work includes five collaborations with director Tim Burton and Johnny Depp. Their first was the animated feature *Corpse Bride* in 2005. In 1997, the actress received Oscar and Golden Globe nominations for playing Kate Croy in *The Wings of the Dove*. She received acclaim for playing Bellatrix Lestrange in a few of the vastly popular *Harry Potter* movies released between 2007 and 2011. As the colorful brothel madam Red Harrington, Bonham

Carter sports a fancy wooden leg with a gun which fires from the shoe. She uses it to help the Masked Man and Tonto against the bad guys.

As in the previous *Lone Ranger* movie, the Indians are against Tonto and the Ranger. But now they are Comanches (as in the 1981 feature), and even endanger our heroes' lives. When they are trapped in the ground, with just their heads protruding and scorpions threatening, it is up to Silver to save the day.

Gil Birmingham, the chief from the earlier TV movie, is now seen as Red Knee, second in tribal command. For this film, the chief was played by Saginaw Grant, who kept reminding me of Floyd Red Crow Westerman's graying Indian chief from *Dances with Wolves* (1990).

Born in 1953, Birmingham began his acting career on an 1986 episode of TV's *Riptide*. In 2005, he was seen as Indian Older Dog Star on four episodes of the miniseries *Into the West*. The actor may be best known for portraying Billy Black in four of the *Twilight* movies between 2008 and 2012. In 2011, he was one of the voices for Gore Verbinski's *Rango*.

Born in England in 1948, Tom Wilkinson first became involved in film and TV during the 1970s. He was one of the unemployed men who stripped for cash in 1997's *The Full Monty*. The following year, he was in the Best Picture Oscar winner *Shakespeare in Love*, playing a theater financier. He won an Emmy and a Golden Globe for his portrayal of Ben Franklin in *John Adams*, a 2008 HBO miniseries. As tycoon Latham Cole in the *Ranger* film, Wilkinson made for a charming yet very dangerous villain. In one scene, his character smacks child Danny Reid across the face. Cole's demise is both welcome and spectacular. Sitting atop one of the train cars with his precious silver, he is crushed and drowned when it spills off the bridge.

William Fichtner and Barry Pepper's screen deaths as his accomplices are also well deserved and spectacular. Each is in a separate train car, one going forward and the other backward on the same track; and the two men then stare at each other in total surprise before the fatal crash.

Born in 1956, Fichtner's first TV acting appearance was on a 1987 episode of the daytime drama *As the World Turns*. One of his early film roles was as a cop in 1992's *Malcolm X*. He gave strong performances in regular TV roles on series programming. He played Sheriff Tom

Underlay in 22 episodes of *Invasion* in the 2005–06 season, and Alex Malone on 59 episodes of *Prison Break* between 2006 and 2009.

Fichtner gave the dirtiest and most violent portrayal of Butch Cavendish to date. Following the Texas Ranger ambush, Butch cuts out Dan's heart with a knife and eats it. Both a powerful and versatile performer, he was also heard as the voice of Butch for 2013's *Disney Infinity* video game. The younger Cavendish briefly seen in the film was played by Travis Hammer, and the younger Cole was played by Steve Corona.

A versatile performer in his own right, Barry Robert Pepper was born in 1970 in Canada. His first recurring TV role was Mick Farleigh on 16 episodes of a Canadian series, *Madison*.

The role of New York Yankee great Roger Maris in the 2001 TV movie *61* earned Barry critical acclaim. He appeared with distinction in two of Tom Hanks' best films: as a sniper in 1998's *Saving Private Ryan* and as a prison guard in the following year's *The Green Mile.*

Pepper's Captain Fuller in *The Lone Ranger* cannot make up his mind which way to turn. He is duped into choosing the wrong side and immediately sets up our hero before a firing squad, but Tonto saves the day. Fuller inadvertently runs a saber through Chief Big Bear in the same sequence.

An impressive array of arrows from the Comanches rains down on Fuller's men here to inadvertently also help Tonto and the Ranger. Unfortunately a Gatling gun is then used by the soldiers to help defeat the Indians.

As the grizzled Collins in the film, Leon Rippy is given a more sympathetic spin than the character received in earlier outings. Yet he is still the traitor who sets up the Rangers for their inevitable doom, despite his later disobedience of Butch's orders to shoot Rebecca and her son.

Rippy was seen in a somewhat sympathetic light as Sgt. William Ward, one of the doomed defenders, in the 2004 film *The Alamo.* Again in 2004, this fine character actor was seen in a regular role on 36 episodes of the Western TV series *Deadwood.* Between 1990 and 2002, Rippy appeared in seven motion pictures for director Roland Emmerich. Included was 2000's *The Patriot,* filmed in Rock Hill, South Carolina, where Leon was born in 1949.

Harry John Newman Treadaway was born in 1984. Like some of the other *Lone Ranger* players, he too was from England. He and twin brother Luke formed a band when they were young; ironically, Harry's film debut in 2005's *Brothers of the Head* was about twins in a rock band. In 2014, Treadaway began playing one of the great horror roles, Dr. Victor Frankenstein, in a TV series called *Penny Dreadful.*

As Frank, one of the more prominent Cavendish gang members, Harry Treadaway cannot help but be a standout. He is not only spirited and full of deadly mischief, but also has a yen for wearing women's clothing. "This ain't what it looks like, mister," he says at one point. I just like them pretty things."

When *The Lone Ranger* opened in U.S. theaters over the July 4, 2013, weekend, it landed in second place with box office earnings of $29.3 million. While it would gross $260.5 million worldwide, its total domestic earnings were but $89.3 million. This is certainly a lot of money, but the film's budget was $225 million. And an additional amount between 150 and 160 million was spent on its marketing campaign. The motion picture therefore was deemed a financial failure.

Newspaper reviews were mixed. On the negative side, *The New York Post* called it a "bloated, misshapen mess," among other things. The *San Jose Mercury* concurred: "In the end, *The Lone Ranger* is one hot mess—an entertaining one, to be sure, but still a mess."

The Boston Herald referred to it as "part spoof, part pastiche" and cited its "spectacular settings" and "colorful characters out of Spaghetti Westerns of yore." *Forbes* magazine ran a glowing review, calling it a "well-written, well-acted, superbly directed adventure story.... It's a wonderful movie!"

There supposedly was some controversy at the production level with casting Johnny Depp as a Native American, probably because of the era of political correctness we all now share. But Depp had stated that he believed Indian blood ran in his family due to a great grandmother. Joseph E. Foy played the boy Tonto, who is duped into sacrificing his tribe for a pocket watch.

One of the best things about *The Lone Ranger* was the interchange between Tonto and the little boy at the Wild West Exhibition. Mason Cook's Will, complete with cowboy hat, outfit, toy guns and the endearing mask, wonderfully plays off the wise old Indian's enchanting storytelling.

For any motion picture, especially one of the magnitude of the 2013 *Lone Ranger*, stunts are an intricate part of the filmmaking process. Over 170 stunt performers were involved on the Western. They included Johnny Depp's stunt double Todd Warren and Armie Hammer's stunt double Jeremy Fitzgerald. The man in charge of the actors' safety was Michael T. Brady.

Prior to filming, Armie Hammer went to a "cowboy camp" to get in shape for his role. He felt it was a real plus. He said that for two weeks, it was "lassos, bullwhips, handguns, horses—every six-year-old's dream."

As an actor, Hamner was undoubtedly inspired by his preparation for the Lone Ranger role. A bit of Texas Ranger history was shared in the beginning of this book to reflect the inspiration for the fictional character.

Epilogue

Never given recognition by *Lone Ranger* creators Fran Striker and George W. Trendle, another true-life Western figure has been given credit for inspiring the Lone Ranger legend: Bass Reeves.

Reeves was born into slavery in 1838, and became a free man when slavery was abolished in 1865. When Federal Judge Isaac Parker made James F. Fagan a marshal of the Indian Territory, he directed him to hire some 200 deputy marshals. A natural for the job, Reeves was a marksman with both pistol and rifle—and he could speak several Indian tongues.

For 32 years, Reeves served as a law enforcer, working in Arkansas, Oklahoma and Texas. After he retired in 1907, he claimed to have made over 3000 arrests; and he shot over a dozen outlaws in self-defense. Reeves died in 1910 of nephritis. He was 71 years old.

Reeves, stalwart and brave, was a factor for inspiring the Lone Ranger. He also inspired a few television episodes, including two in 2015, on *Gunslingers* and *Legends & Lies*. Both cable episodes were titled "Bass Reeves: The Real Lone Ranger."

Reeves' *Gunslingers* show was episode 4 of the second season. On *Legends & Lies*, his was episode 9 of the first season. D.L. Hopkins played Reeves.

Over the years, feature film interest in the life of Bass Reeves has been expressed. At one point, the esteemed Morgan Freeman was interested in portraying the frontier lawman.

Even before creators Trendle and Striker introduced their Masked Man on radio in 1933, the title *The Lone Ranger* was used for two silent shorts, the first in 1920, the other in 1927. The great Western writer Zane Grey wrote his story *The Lone Star Ranger* in 1915 before either of the shorts was made, and over the years it was made into both silent and sound films.

While none of these had a Masked Man with a faithful Indian companion, they did have stories with Texas Rangers. Whether they influenced the Lone Ranger creators cannot be known for sure. But one thing is certain: they all reflected heroes trying to make the West a better place for folks to live. And they were all a part of history.

As a youngster growing up when TV Westerns were all the rage, I recall the sidekicks just as fondly as I do the main heroes. But Jingles with Wild Bill Hickok or Pancho with the Cisco Kid, while certainly helpful, more often were depicted as being humorous. Not so with Jay Silverheels as Tonto. Jay Silverheels' Indian companion seemed to have the same fortitude as the Lone Ranger. Jay did sometimes spoof his own image, including a September 1969 TV guest appearance with Johnny Carson. A sketch with the two has Tonto looking for other employment; it became part of the 1973 record album "Here's Johnny: Magic Moments from *The Tonight Show*."

The lack of total success of the performers who followed Clayton Moore and Jay Silverheels as the Ranger and Tonto is evidence of how indelible their performances as the characters were.

It was not only in film or television that other performers tried to capture Moore and Silverheels' magic. In backyards as a boy with my friends, we played cowboys and Indians, and the first heroes we wanted to be were the Lone Ranger and Tonto.

Indeed we were in our own minds.

Bibliography

Books

Aaker, Everett. *Television Western Players of the Fifties: A Biographical Encyclopedia of All Regular Cast Members in Western Series 1949–1959.* Jefferson, NC: McFarland, 1997.

Brooks, Tim, and Earle Marsh. *The Complete Directory to Prime Time Network and Cable TV Shows, 1946–Present.* New York: Ballantine, 1999.

Buxton, Frank, and Bill Owen. *The Big Broadcast, 1920–1950.* New York: Viking: 1972.

Cline, William C. *Serials-ly Speaking: Essays on Cliffhangers.* Jefferson, NC: McFarland, 1994.

Cox, Mike. *The Texas Rangers Vol. 1: Wearing the Cinco Peso, 1821–1900.* New York: Forge/Tom Doherty, 2008.

Dunning, John. *The Encyclopedia of Old-Time Radio.* New York & Oxford: Oxford University, 1998.

Erickson, Hal. *Television Cartoon Shows: An Illustrated Encyclopedia 1949 through 1993.* Jefferson, NC: McFarland, 2005.

Fagen, Herb. *White Hats and Silver Spurs.* Jefferson NC: McFarland, 1996.

Gelbert, Doug. *Film and Television Locations: A State-by-State Guide.* Jefferson, NC: McFarland, 2002.

Hardy, Phil. *The Encyclopedia of Western Movies.* Minneapolis: Woodbury, 1984.

Hayes, R.M. *The Republic Chapterplays: A Complete Filmography of the Serials Released by Republic Pictures Corporation, 1934–1955.* Jefferson, NC: McFarland, 1991.

Holland, Ted. *B Western Actors Encyclopedia: Facts; Photos and Filmographies for More Than 250 Familiar Faces.* Jefferson, NC: McFarland, 1985.

International Dictionary of Films and Filmmakers, Vol. 2: Directors. 1984. Vol. 3: Actors and Actresses. 1986. Vol. 4: Writers and Production Artists. 1987. Detroit: St. James/Gale.

Lentz, Harris M., III. *Television Western Episode Guide: All United States Series, 1949–1996.* Jefferson, NC: McFarland, 1997.

Lentz, Harris M., III. *Western and Frontier Film and Television Credits, 1903–1995. Vol. 1: Actors and Actresses; Directors, Producers and Writers. Vol. 2: Film Index; Television Index.* Jefferson, NC: McFarland, 1996.

Maltin, Leonard. *The Great American Broadcast.* New York: Dutton/Penguin, 1997.

Maltin, Leonard (Editor). Leonard Maltin's Classic Movie Guide: 2nd edition. New York: Plume/Penguin, 2010.

Marill, Alvin H. *Movies Made for Television: Vol. 4 2000–2004*. Lanham, MD: Scarecrow, 2005.
Moore, Clayton, with Fred Thompson. *I Was That Masked Man*. Dallas: Taylor, 1998.
Nachman, Gerald. *Raised on Radio*. New York: Pantheon, 1998.
Nash, Jay Robert, and Stanley Ralph Ross (Editors). *The Motion Picture Guide: L–M*. Detroit: St. James/Gale, 1986.
Newcomb, Horace (Editor). *Encyclopedia of Television: 2nd Edition. Vol. 2 D–L; Vol. 4 S–Z, Index*. New York; London: Dearborn, 2004.
Reinehr, Robert C., and Jon D. Swartz. *Historical Dictionary of Old-Time Radio*. Lanham, MD: Scarecrow, 2008.
Robinson, Charles M., III. *The Men Who Wear the Star: The Story of the Texas Rangers*. New York: Random House, 2000.
Rothel, David. *Who Was That Masked Man? The Story of the Lone Ranger*. Cranbury, NJ: Barnes; London: Toseloff, 1976
Utley, Robert M. *Lone Star Justice: The First Century of the Texas Rangers*. New York & Oxford: Oxford University, 2000.
Van Hise, James. *The Story of the Lone Ranger*. Las Vegas: Pioneer, 1990.
Witney, William. *In A Door, Into A Fight, Out A Door, Into A Chase*. Jefferson, NC: McFarland, 1996.
Woolery, George W. *Children's Television: The First Thirty-Five Years, 1946–1981. Part I: Animated Cartoon Series*. 1983. *Part II: Live, Film, and Tape Series*. Metuchen, NJ: Scarecrow, 1985.

Internet

americanprofile.com
davycrockettsalmanack.blogspot.com
en.wikipedia.org
filesofjerryblake.com
www.accesshollywood.com
www.amazon.com
www.b-westerns.com
www.classictvhits.com
www.cowboyup.com
www.deppimpact.com
www.hollywoodreporter.com
www.imdb.com
www.melodyranchstudio.com
www.movielocationsplus.com
www.nytimes.com
www.otr.net
www.revolutionsf.com
www.rottentomatoes.com
www.tcm.com
www.texasranger.com
www.westernclippings.com
www.worldbookonline.com

Index